THIS TRAGIC EARTH

THE ART AND WORLD OF RICHARD SHARPE SHAVER

by: Richard Sharpe Shaver
Compiled and Edited by Wm. Michael Mott

Grave Distractions Publications
Nashville, TN

This Tragic Earth:
The Art and World of Richard Sharpe Shaver

by: Richard Sharpe Shaver

Compiled and Edited by Wm. Michael Mott

Grave Distractions Publications
Nashville, Tennessee
www.gravedistractions.com

Cataloging-In-Publication Data
Shaver, Richard Sharpe (Author)
Wm. Michael Mott (Editor)
This Tragic Earth: The Art and World of Richard Sharpe Shaver
ISBN: 978-0-9855991-5-7
Cover Art: Wm. Michael Mott
Internal Layout: Brian Kannard, Grave Distractions Publications

Rogfogo Paintings excerpted from "The Secret World" and material from *Search Magazine* used by permission of Ray Palmer, Jr. Credited photos of Richard S. Shaver provided by Richard Toronto of *Shavertron.* The texts of "Shaver on AbstractArt", "Hideosities", "The Cloud Painter", "The Mystery of Shaver", "The People of Yesterday", and the typescript for "On Rogfogos" provided by Richard Toronto. Shaver interview material from the fanzine *Vampire* #6, June 1946, provided by Gerald W. Page.

Publisher's note: The articles in this text have been reproduced with the exact syntax that appeared in the original texts. Given the condition of original image stock, some images contained within this text are of varying quality. Every effort has been made to faithfully reproduce these images in the highest quality possible in this edition.

Electronic versions of this text are available.
For more information visit:
http://www.gravedistractions.com.

Printed in the USA

TABLE OF CONTENTS

Richard S. Shaver

INTRODUCTION
THE SURREAL REALITY OF RICHARD SHARPE SHAVER

PHOTO:RICHARD TORONTO

What you hold in your hands is a Book of Wonder—one man's wonder, his sense of awe and mystery—a mystery which fascinated readers for fifty years. What you hold is, in part, a facsimile of one of the rare lost notebooks of Richard Sharpe Shaver (1907-1975), fiction writer, non-fiction writer, artist, poet, dreamer, and philosopher. And his philosophy is best summed up in one word:

Beware.

Beware of the deros (detrimental robots), the subhuman/superhuman degenerates below.

Beware of their flying machines, which Shaver described in identical detail before the first "official" flying saucer reports came to light.

Beware of modern society, a demented world secretly run by subterranean dementos, and at the mercy of their manipulative and mind destroying rays.

Beware of the Past, when the moon fell, the oceans rose, monsters and human-animal hybrids roamed, the sun grew evil, the ancients left the planet, and their refugees—our ancestors—dug into the ground to survive. Some eventually came out into daylight again, but the others remained below, from whence they secretly rule the world today, both devolved and evolved, and as far removed from modern humans as we are from chimpanzees.

Beware of human arrogance, folly, egotism, short-sightedness, warmongering, environmental destruction, and general stupidity.

Beware of all of these things, because all of these things and more were encompassed by Richard Shaver's worldview, and he was not bashful about sharing his opinions, whether they appeared in a science-fiction fantasy tale about the pre-cataclysmic world for magazines like *Amazing* or *Fantastic* (often hinted at as "truth" by the author), or in "serious" and sincere literature warning of the *Hidden World* below; or in the lessons he found in his famous "rock books," wherein which he found images that he often turned into paintings.

From his explosion on the publishing scene in December of 1943, until the early seventies, Shaver published his tales of elder world wonder and terror. Thousands of people around the world wrote letters and literature that supported Shaver's claims. Yet throughout most of this time, Shaver largely worked with one editorial dynamo—his original editor at *Amazing*, who had pulled his letter from a waste-basket, and created a pulp-era sensation—the same man who saw Shaver's work into print in at least half a dozen magazines and publications, including *Fate*, *Search*, and *The Hidden World*. That man was Raymond A. Palmer.

Ray Palmer has been vilified for his work with Shaver, for his editorial collaborations, for his promotion of the "Shaver Mystery". In science-fiction circles, many have had negative things to say about Shaver, whom some consider to have been mentally unbalanced, but as many have vilified Palmer, whom they regard as having exaggerated Shaver's stories and taken advantage of a delusional man. Yet, as the present tome attests, Shaver's ideas needed no embellishment or addition—and as for Ray Palmer, well, RAP, as he was known to his fans, got quite a bad rap indeed. Ray helped Shaver make a living when he otherwise might not have been socially functional enough to stick with regular employment. And he probably would never have developed as a writer and artist of the type he did, if he'd remained a welding-gun operator suffering from what modern medicine would almost certainly have diagnosed as paranoid schizophrenia—given his apparent state of mind the first day he heard the "voices from the underworld", completely by accident and unbidden, triggered by the vibrations and perhaps the electromagnetic field generated by the equipment with which he was working.

The interest from the art world in Shaver's work that is now occurring eluded him entirely during his lifetime.

Interest in his work, from different perspectives, can be found in the following circles:

1. The Art Crowd (where he's now hailed as an "Outsider Artist")
2. The Science Fiction Crowd
3. The Mysteries/Unexplained/UFO Crowd.

As far as I know, his is the only work, which, as a body, covers all that territory. Whereas some might see the value of one piece out of the rogfogo packet as an art piece, for instance, someone like Richard Toronto (Shaver friend and renowned publisher of *Shavertron*) would see the value of keeping everything together for historical purposes. As a phenomenon, though, Richard Shaver encompasses all of these areas, and more or less reflects a time in American history marked by cold war paranoia, the emergence of new folklore and even superstition systems, and also the rise of science fiction from a "dirty" and disrespected genre, to something that in many ways formed our pop culture and influenced society.

The material in this book, for the most part, was sent to Ray Palmer. There was the book itself, *This Tragic Earth*, along with a packet of photos of sliced pieces of rock, through which Shaver had exposed light onto photographic paper. The "rock books", as Shaver called them, he also called rokphotos and rogfogos, the latter name probably derived from cognates in his legendary Mantong Alphabet, the ancestral language of humanity and related beings. Oh yeah, it nearly slipped my mind—the *Mantong*, and the story that went with it, *I Remember Lemuria*, were what started the whole ball rolling back in '43. So, going back to the first paragraph of this introduction, add "linguist" or "philologist" to the list of Shaver's self-taught accomplishments.

It will be noticed that Shaver's original *This Tragic Earth* mock-up is missing all text on page 7. Why? Only Shaver could say. This gap is filled with other material for purposes of continuity. The final version of the booklet may have ended up as the self-published piece *Giant Evening Wings,* which Shaver sold by mail in the early '70s. In addition to the booklet and photos, there was also a letter that Shaver wrote to Palmer after an unpleasant trip to a local hospital. In this missive we can see the full scope of Shaver's alternative worldview, and the way in which it permeated every thought, every aspect of his life. There are also some rare rogfogo tips, hints, and commentary from Shaver, which appeared in *Search Magazine* and *The Psychic Observer*, along with an interview in the science fiction fanzine *The Alien Critic*, from May 1974.

Richard S. Shaver and one of his "picture rocks"

Many extra rogfogo images are presented, sectionally and with some scattered throughout. These are strange, sometimes frightening, weird, and bizarre, and are taken from smaller sections of the larger rock book slice photos that he had sent to Palmer. These images are eerie and surreal—their presence in the rock photos defies rational explanation. Some of them would seem to be too strange to be a result of mere coincidence, or of the tendency of the human mind to find patterns (particularly facial patterns) in random data. Often they resemble the tortured convolutions and figures found in the work of Hieronymous Bosch. As Shaver described the process of the ancestors of the deros (and ourselves) who "layered" these pictures in the rocks, he claimed that they were meant to be playable recordings of 3D projections, if one just had the technology. In other words, he was describing a type of crystal holography, although he didn't use that terminology. Since most or many of his rogfogo photos were fairly small, they probably all contain such shapes and faces. If their owners would scan them and then rotate them in every direction in Photoshop, zooming in, they would find even more hidden images (whether hidden by the dero or by Shaver himself, only Shaver would have known). Ultimately, the truth or non-truth behind these images, and behind the ideas of Richard Sharpe Shaver, are up to the reader to decide for him- or herself.

Now, thanks to the hard work of a few men like Brian Tucker and others, Shaver is being hailed in some circles as an artistic genius, an "Outsider Artist" who never received the acclaim he so vainly (it seems) sought during his lifetime. His paintings and drawings are on display in galleries in New York and Los Angeles, yet he could barely give them away when he was alive. It is of small doubt that Shaver would say that this was all due to "dero tamper", to the interference and twisted sense of humor of the degenerates below, who control the minds of art critics as thoroughly as they do the minds of other men and women.

Whatever the case, Richard Sharpe Shaver was, in his own way, a visionary: a science-fiction mystic (he hated the term "mystic", though), a dreaming materialist, and an artistic, poetic soul of rare talent and sensibility. Only now, after he's gone, does the world slowly, dimly, begin to realize what it has lost, as if awakening from the stupefying effects of a dero telaug machine.

Better late than never.

Wm. Michael Mott, June 2006
Author of *Caverns, Cauldrons, and Concealed Creatures*
Pulsifer: A Fable, and *Land of Ice, A Velvet Knife*

Publisher's Note: The following images are from *This Tragic Earth.* Every attempt has been made to render these images as clearly as possible. However, the manuscript for Shaver's work was made in the days before digital imaging was accessible to the public. The goal has been to preserve Shaver's original work visually as best as possible from the original source. Unfortunately, some of the images are not as visually crisp as others. A transcript of *This Tragic Earth,* with the original Shaver pictures, follows this section that makes for an easier read.

1.

THIS TRAGIC EARTH

In the days when the phrase "Giant Evening Wings" was first used they were already used to the idea of the end of life coming for them all. They had been raised with the fact of the approaching capture of the moon known to everyone.

Some poet had turned the phrase to make the coming destruction less horrible and easier to live with, perhaps. One gathers that the ever thought of doomsday was no new idea and that they accepted it.

One point I wish to make clear is that doomsday is coming again for us all, that it is right overhead and quite visible on moonlit nights. It is the moon, which has fallen over and over upon the earth since the first capture.

"Giant Evening Wings" are coming for us all in this era, just as surely as they came for those long gone people of that Elder World.

Once you get the fact quite clear in your head, a slow anger against the science of astronomy and all of our sciences that can have such a burden overhead without being conscious of it or telling us about it....is born and grows a little right along. This anger against the numbed minds of our scientists is a normal and healthy anger. If they cant figure out the orbit and velocity of our moon and know its going to fall why do they call themselves "astronomers" ?

Since everything points to the moon having billiarded off earth at least seven times in the past, how is it they dont even know it fell once?

This whole perspective of science as a sort of blind, deaf and dumb posturing by men quite unable to determine any of the facts of life until they are struck on the head by them is very disconcerting when you first discover it.

The presence of the ancient library of rock books is one of these disconcerting discoveries that exposes this deaf, dumb and blind character of our vaunted science.

Even to bring up the subject of the pre-deluge in any way in any place proves quite impossible. WHY? Because our so wonderful science hasn't yet sanctioned the idea of one deluge.

Somehow they decided, a couple of hundred years ago, that "science" was not favorably inclined toward the biblical deluge and from that time on the deluge was called a "local inundation" in all "scientific texts". And this in spite of the fact that all digs and all investigations of older exposed rocks and earth showed that there had been seven separate wide spread inundations, any one of which had been severe enough to have earned the title of the "Biblical Deluge".

This formulation of scientific policy toward ideas is what we have come to accept as "science" when in fact it is not science, but blind custom.

to accept as science when in fact it i s not science, but blind custom. Science is a concept in our minds, but in fact in actuality it is really an adherence to outmoded ideas as it acts, and affects our lives and as a cönsor in that it affects what is printed and broadcast. There is in fact no organized body of custom worshippers as we are apt to think of "science".

I wouldn't even think of it, except that it stands between me and any possible way of telling the people of the world about moon-falls and their frequency, the imminent approach of still another fall, and about the rock libraries that can open the door of escape.

This door of escape stands openmouthed, awaiting us...it is the way, the science, the methods and specifications of ships...by which many of those elder races, at least before the first moon-fall, evacuated earth.

A thing that stands between a way of escape for a planet full of people who will surely die without it... is not "science", but so many think so it is ridiculously like science.

If they will hear, if they will look and see, if they will do something about the optical problems of reading the rock books of the first great races...then many of the same type of evacuation ships may yet be built before the next moonfall. But "science" doesnt "believe" in moon-falls, biblical floods, or in any of the most important facts about man; his past, and in this case, his ominous and non-istant future.

How to tell mankind about the books his ancient ancestors left lying about has been my main objective for nearly fifteen years. Between me and the public I have found a barrier of quite impassable dimensions,, made up of secretaries whose "science" consisted of learning shorthand and typing, receptionists whose sole qualifiations seem to be well modulated smiles calculated carefully to the cut of the coat, and of men whose sole mental content seems to be an ability to estimate the dollar getting abilities of those they meet.

I have yet to find a human being really interested and understanding of the nature of the message and the real need for action.

One can sympathize with Noah and his ark, and his sad exclsuion of all the people who failed to help him build the ark. But I didnt set out to emulate Noah, I was only trying to give a few students the keys to a great library of the far past.

It was only later that I was able to get from the rock books the great facts about the flood, the moon as its cause, and the infinite correctness of the work of Immanuel Velikovsky.

Well, its their funeral and its their loss. Its their choice of ignorance above wisdom, of sloth above industry and drowning before shipbuilding. Like Noah, it saddens me but there really isnt much I can do about it, short of beating them over the head with a rock book.

Ancient peoples made a number of photos, or photo-projection-paintings (or Boh-Pogo pictures) (in their language) of the coming down of the moon. Here is one.

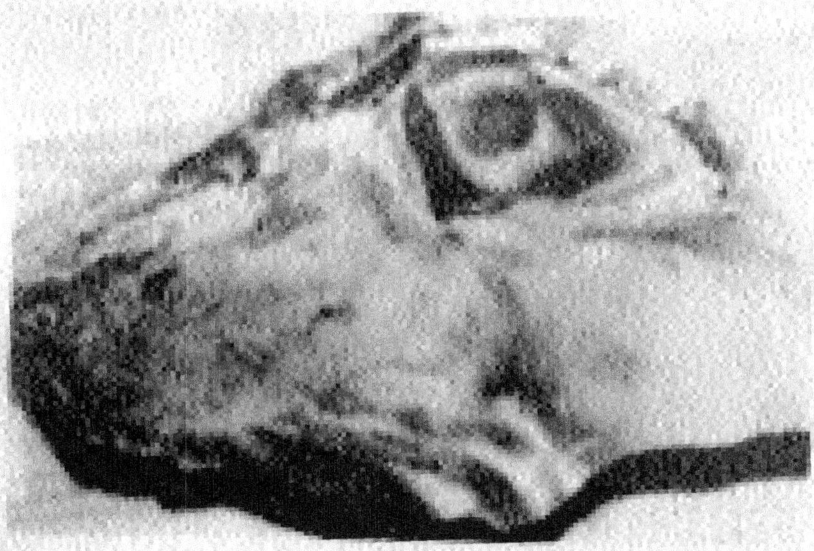

This was about all a lot of inhabitants saw of their own doom as it smashed down through the clouds and pulled their own oceans heaven high.

"The Fall" meant that the moon lost its own oceans, its own air and rocks and loose earth to the world when it bounced off and on.

On and up and out into a new orbit went the moon, but not the people and the beasts of Mother Earth. They lay dead and buried in the mud of their own ocean's bottoms where it had been pulled across the land, buried and smashed beneath the endless fall from the moon; the oceans and the air and the rocks and surface earth of the moon cane down in endless torrents of mud and water. The huge forests of earth were splintered into smashed piles of future coal and mud.

And the ancient cities of old earth, many of them built out of rock-books, were scattered over the world as tidal wave rubble, pushed by the tidal wave movements round and round the earth under the falling moon.

The Mer-people of the oceans, lifted on high with their own ancient oceans and then smashed down into the mud and lava of the new-opened volcanos... were dead and vanished forever from the world.

Science can say it never happened, but any curious child can find the rubble of old earth's cities nearly anywhere he looks. The rubble of wonder cities, age-old in a tradition of true science. Little theater stones shaped like a concert shell, in which the warmth of the hand alone is enough to make the age-old pictures move again. Tiny book stones no bigger than a thimble, that once gave off magnificent color-pictures when placed in a projector. Huge boulder picture stones with life-size human figures in them. Shoe-makers lasts that one could still make a shoe over. .Stone t ype cast of liquids that hardened into the letters of long ago. Flat stones once used for printing color-po ters that will still print if inked. Buttons with little cast designs on them that long ago held their coats shut.

speaks
with
forked
tongue
photo

large profile
covers
height of
print..
all large pic
tures are made
up of smaller

every face of
white has a
black to contrast
it ..and vice
versa

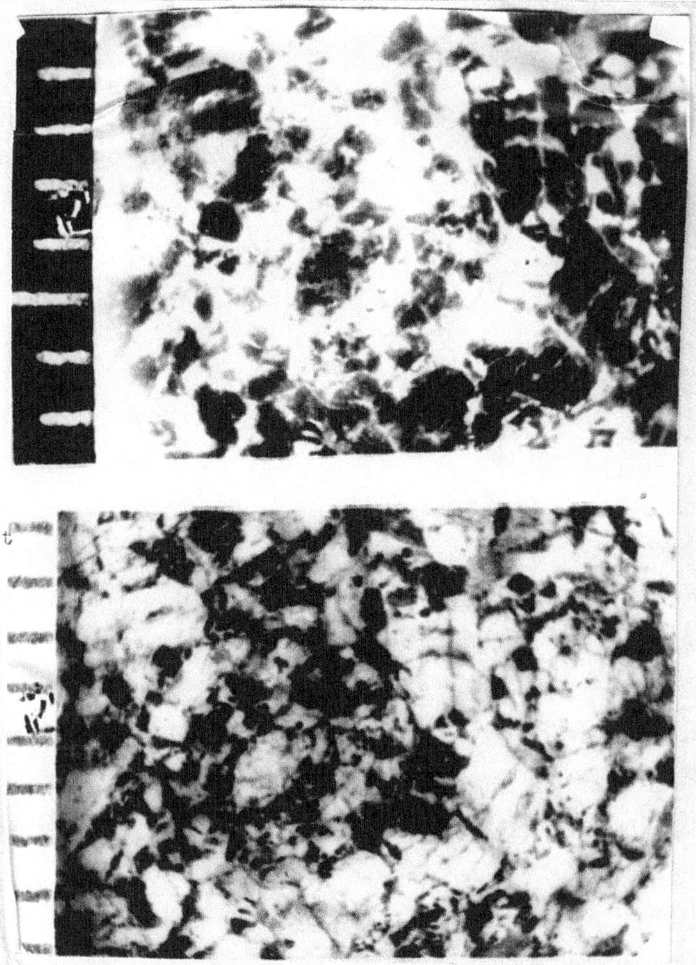

Rap..if you think my prints are bad or obscure or puzzling
why then take a real good look at a page full of Picasso prints
they are far far more o bscure and puzzling, and worse art by far...
and whats more..these are infinitely less childish in what message does
get across

One way to display these prints is to print a Picasso print of the wilder
kind (aren't theyall) and comment that Shaver rock photos are more
intriguing and more thought provoking and even less puzzling by far

isn't thinking correctly about such matters as mass, orbital velocity and spiral orbits.

Earth is just emerging from periods of time called the "Dark Ages". Science has itself a residue of dark ignorant dictums left over from those dark ages.

The cause of those ages of ignorance and darkness is just overhead, shining down with its reflected light borrowed from the sun.

The moon was not always there. When the moon came, it plunged the earth into darkness, the darkness of death and destruction and world-wide blankets of mud and rubble, sand and gravel and the piled boulders of ancient cities so old even then no man knew their beginnings.

BUT we dont need to go on being ignorant victims of a wayward globe of rock. We dont have to submit to this world-wide ignorance of our own beginnings.

NOW we have the libraries left by the people of the pre-deluge world. They CAN be read.

They are encyclopedic, we can determine the exact number of scales on a mermaid's arm, the precise number of ribs in Adam's off-ox, if so inclined, just by a little expert work on the rock books.

But it will take more than one Shaver with his camera and saw. It will take teams of genuine scientists, rather than the fuddy frauds we now accept as scientists.

It will take the kind of men and the wealth of equipment used in putting the Apollo crews on the moon.

And it will take the same kind of determination and decision and action.

It will take a little doing, in teams.

9.

And so, leaving all that, lets think about the phrase "The Fall". The dark ages have left us a lot of singular documentation that indicates "The Fall" is a referende to the Fall of Satan and all his Angels from (of all things) GRACE!

About the only real sense I can get out of all that documentation is that the probable name for the moon when it was a well known planet going round the sun was "Satan", a planet.

When the last of the rock books was written, after the fall had destroyed the ancient ways and most of the ancient original people, the phrase "The Fall" meant one thing alone. That thing was "The Fall of the Moon."

I gave you one of their depictions of the event, a photo of a slice of one of their rock books.

(Oddly enough, the outermost planet of the solar system is named Pluto.)

According to modern descriptions of volcanic action during these world cataclysms, many new volcanos were formed and all the old ones burst into new activity. The whole atmosphere of earth was permeated with sulphurous odors for centuries... and those are not my words, I will try to locate the quote for you.

But, in order to understand what seven separate moon-falls have done to earth, you had better read "Earth in Upheaval" by Velikovsky from cover to cover. No few quotes out of context can have the proper impact of the tremendous assembly of facts he gives.

Just why Velikovsky skirts the fact

of moon-fall I cant fathom, unless in truth he leans toward the reversal of the polarity of earth as a prime cause, or the shifting of the axis of earth as a prime cause.

Myself, I see the whole series of catastrophes which "Earth in Upheaval" substantiates and describes so successfully as results of moon-fall, and the reversal of polarity and the shift in the axis as results of impact with the moon. Mainly this is my view, and I cant understand why anyone needs another prime cause when the moon looms so low and so huge overhead every evening as it rises on the horizon.

To my mind, the unlike poles of the moon magnet clicked together at impact, and the only reason we dont have them still stuck together is that same reversal as earth turned topsy turvy on impact. This threw the poles into LIKE positions of repellance, and the moon moved on into its new orbit because it was freed of the magnetic attraction.

But then I am only a layman, and such matters are really beyond me.

That the moon fell more than once is to me quite obvious, and when the digs reveal seven separate wide destructions I assume they were due to seven moon-falls.

I really dont need the moon to fall on me to take the hint, I get that feeling just by looking up at night.

The quotes and mentionings of the many scientists as they discuss the ice ages and lava flows and dust clouds over centuries of time seem to me so much beating of a dead horse. Why

11.

cant they just look up and see that huge round accident waiting to happen again?

To my mind, and remember its a layman's mind, a scientific theory is some-a scientist invents to keep from seeing the obvious and doing something about it, like real work.

For instance, about ten years ago I wrote to a very scientific gentleman, the Editor of Analog... about the rock book pictures , for some assistance in photographing and documenting their very obvious existence.

At that time I had neither a camera nor any lenses but ordinary reading glasses of the cheap four inch kind.

He immediately went into the scientific theory stance and opined that since all such pictures were "accidentals" there wasn't any need for his work, but that he would do some for $50 a day.

Since I was broke as usual I didn't have a lot to say.

It is my theory that most scientific theories are like that...an easy wayout of a difficult job.

That is, too many scientists find it more practical to theorize than to ascertain the exact facts.

I remember one scientist explaining away a mammoth tooth I showed him by telling me that mammoths nor mastodons "has ever been found in Wisconsin."

It was almost exactly a week later that a steam shovel in Madison, the capital of Wisconsin, where he lived, uncovered a perfect mammoth skull. He would never have heard about that, I suppose , if some ignorant reporter hadn't put the photo into the Madison newspaper. I suppose the reporter hasn't heard about the scientist.

To this poor layman, all scientists who puzzle and puzzle through endless volumes of stilted prose about the mysterious causes of earths so obvious and so numerous world wide cataclysms are typical scientists, who cant see the forest because they are studying a tree.

To me, the nearest and most obvious cause is the first one to examine. And I really cannot understand why they have all been so busy puzzling over the causes of world wide cataclysm with the moon sailing overhead?

But th en I am a man who spent nearly fifteen years trying to get one scientist to look at just one rock, really look, without the slightest success.

Every one of them came up with an excuse to avoid getting out a microscope or a magnifier, the while he labeled his voluminous excuses for not doing anything at all with the very scientific term...his theory!

Personally I will take a bricklayer any day. At least he knows that if a brick falls on your head, it hurts.

Now you know why this book is called "The Layman's Atlantis". That means it is for people who can have a cause and an effect without demanding a theory.

I once sent an artifact bearing very interesting and artistic designs on it to the Smithsonian. They wrote me a letter asking for 55 cents to ship back my "boulder". Now even I knew a rock that small is not a boulder.

I sent the same rock to a photo-curio shop in New York to photograph the ancient pre-ice-age art on it. T,ey did so, and sent me my very first B&W slides of pre-deluge art, very interesting to me. I subsequently sold that same rock to a fan of mine for $25 as an artifact. But, to the Smithsonian it was a boulder, bare of all signifigance. I have had my own suspicions about all scientists ever since.

Personally I actually think they didnt know the difference between a boulder and a small rock, in fact, and didn't actually mean to cast aspersions on my artifact.

There is in fact a blind spot in all over-educated people, I have learned. They have an opinion a man is less intelligent if he hasn't spent most of his life in a school.

My own opinion about that is that a man who has been helped to walk all his life doesn't know how to walk alone.

But there you have an opinion that is like all opinions, a substitute for the real facts. It was real scientists who put the Apollo into orbit around the moon. They weren't working with theories or opinions.

Now if I could just get one of my boulders into their hands, they might find out it was a rock more worthwhile than the ones they brought from the moon. Its my opinion we have endless tons of moon rocks already, that fell when the whole surface of the moon fell on earth... the first moon-fall, that is.

How to show them a moon-rock from the sands of Wisconsin is the problem, for me as insuperable as the first flight to the moon seemed back when they started the Apollo project. It seems my moon-rocks are boulders. But I am only a layman.

One day I will meet a real scientist and I will find it is possible to tell them about moon-rocks already on earth for a long , long time. Or will they have a theory to keep from bending over and picking up one of those so-heavy boulders?

But then, right now I'm writing instead of putting my new microscope adapter on my microscope so I can take some pictures. Maybe they have to write books to make a living is why they cant get any real work done?

While I didn't start out to emphasize the moon-fall theory over any other aspect of the fate of the Elder World, it is crucial. Mainly its crucial because its what happened, and I dont know how to tell it as if it might have happened some other way just to please some people I dont like anyway.

Velikovsky in the final pages of"Earth in Upheaval" draws a picture of the old astronomy as a theoretical picture of the celestial mechanism "wound up to go on forever". He states that "this picture is based upon a mechanistic view of the universe which considers magnetism not at all!"

He goes on to explain that sun observers have noted that solar prominences repel each other actively (something I predicted 25 years ago in science-fiction writings) and that many another phenomenon in astronomical work can only be studied and understood by including magnetic forces and polarities...etc.

All of which he adds up to mean that astronomy is fallible and makes very grave errors that can only be explained

15.

by unincluded magnetic forces which are nevertheless active and powerful in spite of the ignoring attitude of "astronomy".

Bravo to Velikovsky, he actually said it!

But I want to point out that the moon is in stable orbit only because the poles parallel earth's poles at present. What would happen if the poles of the moon drifted so that one attracted one more than the other... or vice versa? Unlikes attract and likes repel doesn't really require solar flare observation to notice, does it?

Velikovsky's concept of earth cataclysms caused by the advent of a passing comet of large size is valid enough as the comet would only need to shift the attitude of the moon enough to point one pole toward earth more than it does now, to have extremely powerful forces come into play.

The point I want to make is that the moon's orbital stability actually depends upon quite other forces than only gravity and velocity in orbit.

In Velikovsky's analyses he has the series of catastrophes caused by the entry of a large comet.

To my mind you don't need a comet's entry to have the catastrophes inevitable and frequent. You only need a moon that lets its magnetic poles drift into alignment with earth's in such a way that likes repel and unlikes attract forcibly enough to cause further drift and further magnetic forces to result...etc.

In other words moon's attitude to earth's poles is most probably the

16.

determing factor in moon's orbital deviations in the past and will be the cause of orbital failure in the future as well.

Why Velikovsky skirts this obvious cause of moon-falls as well as the moon-falls in his writings I cannot fathom unless he has such a hearty respect for the venom and non-co-operation of offended scientists that he simply cannot state the meanings of the observed catastrophes... its too much for me.

To me its obvious that astronomy has mastered the art of the sin of ommission in ignoring the moon as well as the biblical deluge and the seven cultures of earth in the past that were destroyed by the moon-falls.

To me Fort has the whole astronomical world fairly well analyzed in his chapters on astronomy. What Fort would have to say with one of my rock books in his hands I would like to hear.

Moon-rocks as well as the artifacts of seven dead cultures litter the hills and moraines and cut-banks of half the world... and we send a rocket to the moon to get a moon-rock.

My feelings are really that "science" is the art of non-observation!

The presence of unobserved rock books in nearly every rock pile on earth leads me to believe they will always manage to make mistakes in preference to doing some actual observational work in ascertaining the truth about anything.

So, if you want to feel safe under that gibbous moon you read some old astronomy books which place everything in the sky held there by very well balanced forces.

But if you want to know what happened

to the vanished cultures whose books are available to anyone who looks for them on almost any hillside ... you read Velikovsky with the mental reservation that he was at great pains not to offend the great cult of "science" and didn't quite make it, anyway.

I once asked a curator of a large municipal museum why he hung certain copies as genuine, and he told me that he couldn't afford to offend the people who had presented them.

If you read Velikovsky carefully you cant help but visualize some very dignified idiots.

With that moon hanging overhead every night I feel we should offend someone.

It could matter, weightily!

* * *

THIS IS A PAINTING MADE BY PROJECTING A SLICE OF A ROCK BACK ON TO A SENSITIZED CANVAS. THEN I PAINT COLOR ON THE PICTURE. I PUT IT HERE TO ACQUAINT YOU WITH THE STYLE OF ART, & THE HUMOR IN THE PICTURES THAT FILL ROCK BOOKS.

CHAPTER

Speaking of [illegible]

did you ever really look at one? They are covered with the most marvelous raised pictorials!

What's more, the pictures go all the way through the rock! Impossible, but true.

The really weird thing about rock book, after I knew something about them from several years of study of them, was [illegible] their contents.

The really weird thing about rocks is the fact that the whole population of this old earth has managed to ignore them!

How did they manage this piece of tom-foolery?

But a little library research reassured me. It seems that as late as 1700 sailors took gazing stones to sea with them to pass the time in the forecastle!

And that not much earlier the last of the troubadours was still singing from stones he carried with him!

And that not much earlier than that gazing stones were an article of commerce. So the total population of earth has not been entirely blind, always.

This is the "rock" from which the monster on opposite page was enlarged. You can find him left center.

To get the most out of these complex montages of monsters, mermaids, and other lively and ungentle creatures of the far past...you must learn to tilt and turn your rock slowly to let the light o utline each face and figure... for that is how they were made to be seen. This is not a difficult skill, but it does have to be learned

You had better learn to collect these for yourself while they are still available on mountain slopes and dry river beds... for civilization has a way of destroying all traces of the past... just as the strip mines are destroying the lovely mountains of Kentucky.

One day these despised "rocks" will bring prices no diamond ever did...for they have a vast value beyond all the superficial glitter of any diamond.

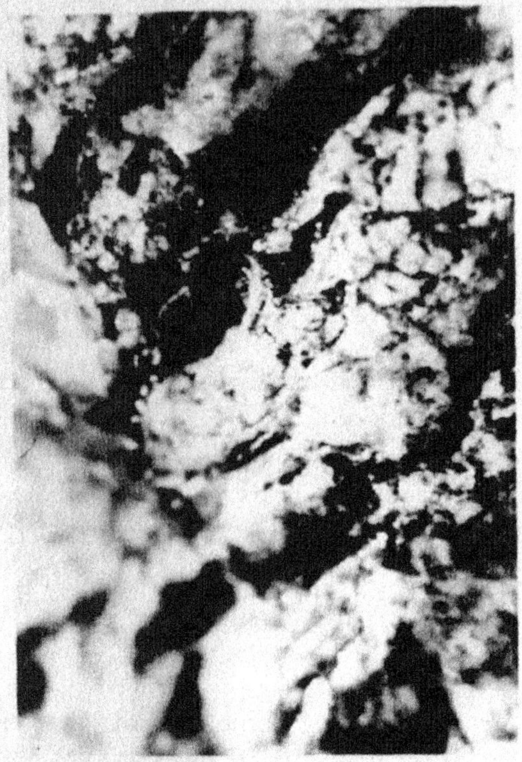

This mons ter's head is one of a great many on this rock, which is shown at left. If you look just left of center on the rock, you find the reptilian head of which this is an enlargement.

This whole rock is a montage of brawling reptilian monsters of several varieties. If you are interested in the age of dinosaurs as it really was, and not as it is sometimes misrepresented in mistaken textsbooks, then you can see it for yourself in such rocks as this.

TO ME, THE FACE ABOVE IS PLAINER

than the photo of myself, below, holding the rock from which the photo above was taken.

That rock is the most valuable object on our world, and its kind are totally ignored by our so-wonderful science that put a man on the moon and brought back fifty pounds of moon rocks. I wonder if they will mangge to ignore all the images in the rocks from the moon, too?

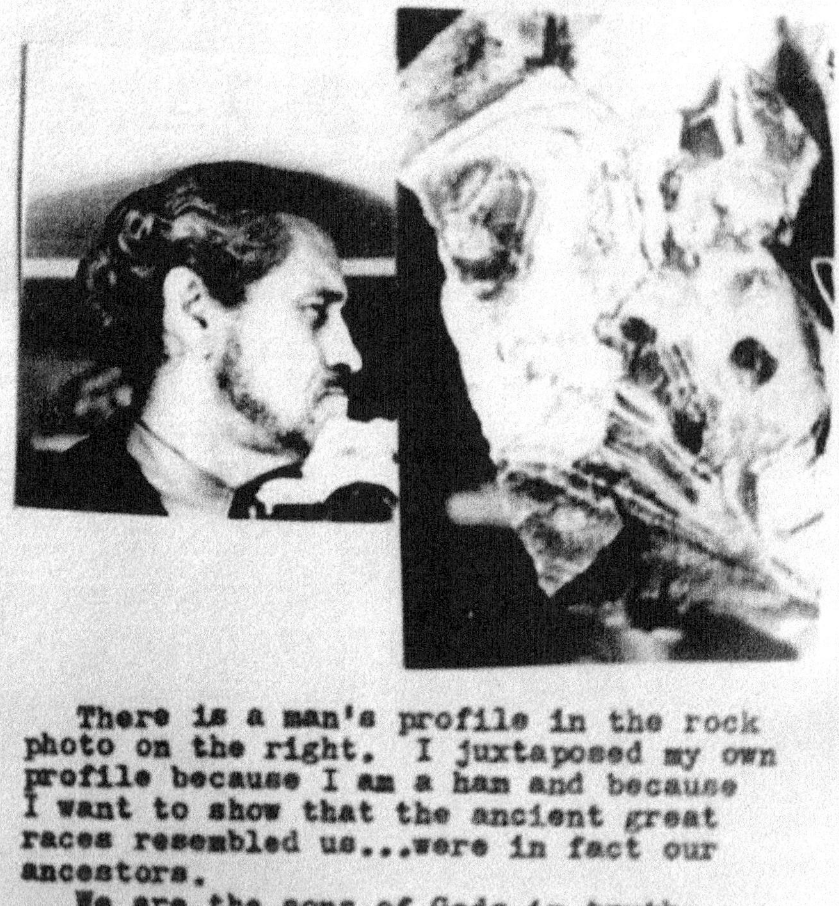

There is a man's profile in the rock photo on the right. I juxtaposed my own profile because I am a ham and because I want to show that the ancient great races resembled us...were in fact our ancestors.

We are the sons of Gods in truth. Once before the moon fell our kind multiplied through all space...and our relatives are out there, awaiting us.

Why dont we know this?

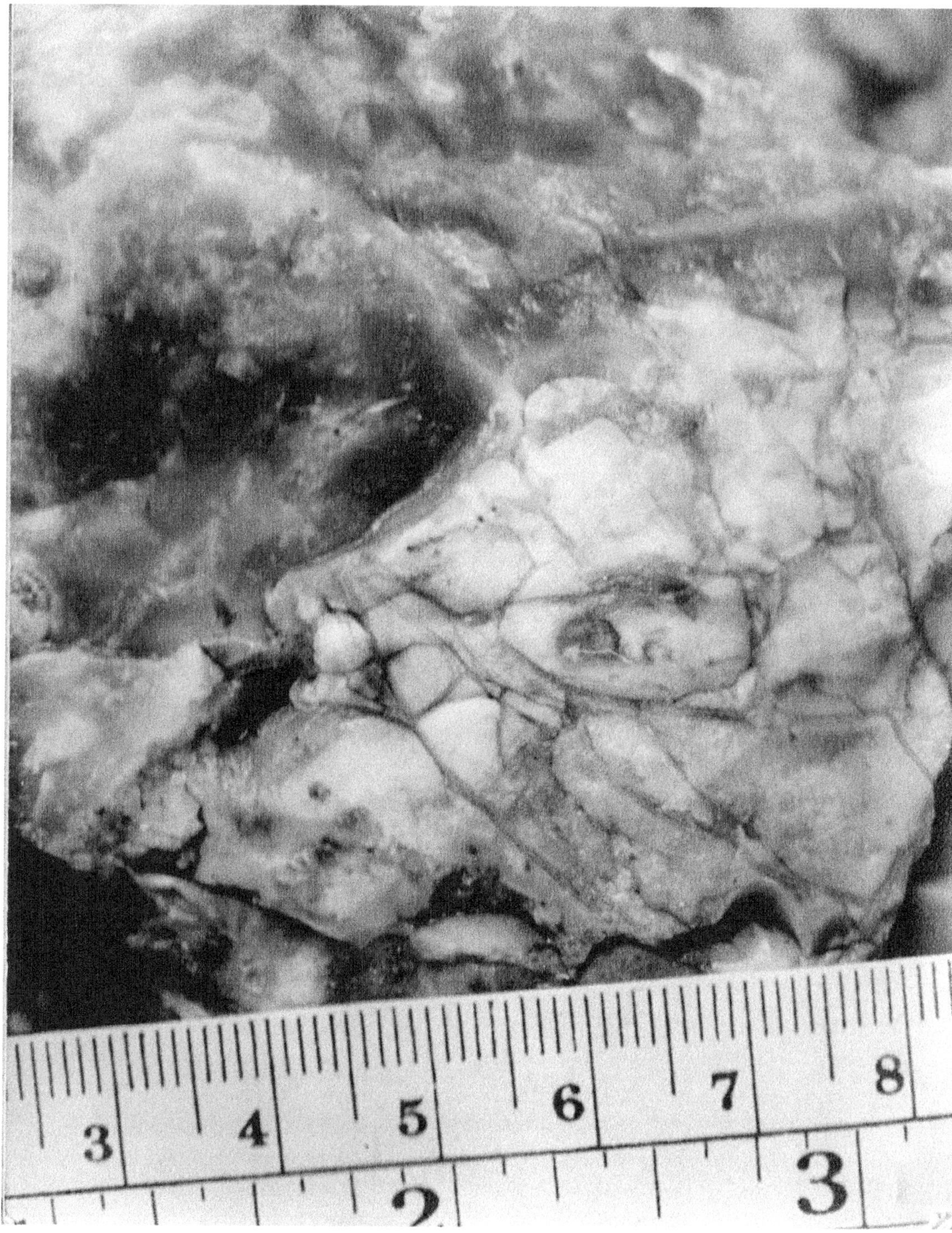
3 4 5 6 7 8
2 3

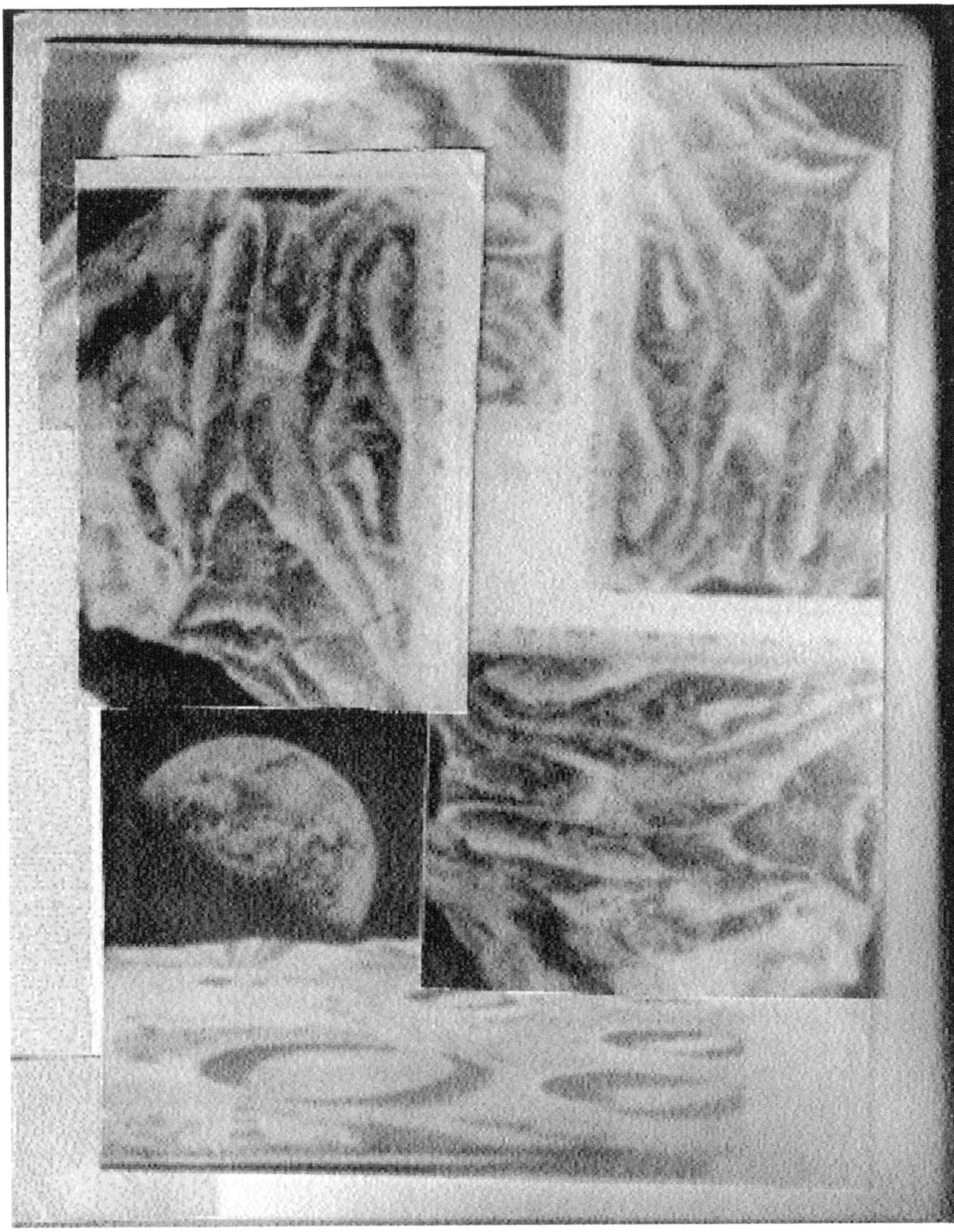

THIS TRAGIC EARTH

Publisher's Note: The following text is taken directly from the manuscript of *This Tragic Earth*. All text is as it appears exactly within that manuscript. Shaver's images have been placed as close as possible to the original locations within the manuscript.

In the days when the phrase "Giant Evening Wings" was first used they were already used to the idea of the end of life coming for them all. They had been raised with the fact of the approaching capture of the moon known to everyone.

Some poet had turned the phrase to make the coming destruction less horrible and easier to live with, perhaps. One gathers that the ever thought of doomsday was no new idea and that they accepted it.

One point I wish to make clear is that doomsday is coming again for us all, that is right overboard and quite visible on moonlit nights. It is the moon, which has fallen over and over upon the earth since the first capture.

"Giant Evening Wings are coming for me all in this era, just as surely as they came for those long gone people of that Elder World.

Once you get the fact quite clear in your head, a slow anger against the science of astronomy and all of our motions that can have such a burden overhead without being conscious of it or telling us about it... in horn and grows a little right along. The anger against the numbed minds of our scientists is a normal and healthy anger. If they cant figure out the orbit and velocity of our moon and know its going to fall why do they call themselves "astronomers"?

Since everything points to the moon having billiarded off earth at least seven times in the past, how is it they don't even know it fell once?

The whole perspective of science as a sort of blind, deaf, and dumb pouring by men unable to determine any of the facts of life until they are struck on the head by them is very disconcerting when you first discover it.

The presence of the ancient litany of rock books is one of these disconcerting discoveries that exposes this deaf, dumb, and blind character of our vaunted sciences.

Even to bring up the subject of the pre-deluge in any way in any place erodes quite impossible. WHY? Because our so wonderful science hasn't yet mentioned the idea of one deluge.

Somehow they decided a couple of hundred years ago, that "science" was not favorably inclined toward the biblical deluge and from that time on the deluge was called a "local inundation" in all "scientific texts". And this is in spite of the fact that all digs and all investigations of older exposed rocks and earth showed that there had been seven separate wide spread inundation inundations, any one of which had been newer enough to have harmed the title of the "Biblical Deluge".

This formulation of scientific policy toward ideas is what we have come to accept as "science" when in fact it is not science, but blind custom, to accept as science when in fact it is not science, but blind custom. Science is a concept in our minds, but in fact in actuality it is really an adherence to outmoded ideas as it acts, and affects our lives and as a censor in that is affects what is printed and broadcast. There is in fact no organized body of custom worshippers as we are apt to think of "science".

I wouldn't even think of it, except that it stands between me and any possible way of telling the people around the world about moon-falls and their frequency, the imminent approach of still another fall, and about the rock libraries that can open the door of escape.

This door of escape stands open-mouthed, awaiting us...it is the way, the science, the methods and specifications of ships...by which many of those elder races, at least before the first moon-fall, evacuated earth.

If they will hear, if they will look and see, if they will do something about the optical problems of reading the rock books of the first great races...then many of the same type of evacuation ships may yet be built before the next moon-fall. But "science" doesnt "believe" in moon-falls, biblical floods, or in any of the most importation facts about man; his past, and in this case, his ominous and non-instant future.

How to tell mankind about the books his ancient ancestors left lying about has been my main objective for nearly fifteen years. Between me and the public I have found a barrier of quite impassable dimensions,, made up of secretaries whose "science" consisted of learning shorthand and typing, receptionists whose sole qualifications seem to be well modulated smiles calculated carefully to the cut of the coat, and of men whose sole mental content seems to be an ability to estimate the dollar getting abilities of those they meet.

I have yet to find a human being really interested and understanding of the nature of the message and the real need for action.

One can sympathize with Noah and his ark, and his sad exclusion of all the people who failed to help him build the ark. But I didnt set out to emulate Noah, I was only trying to give a few students the keys to a great library of the far past.

It was only later that I was able to get from the rock books the great facts about the flood, the moon as its cause, and the infinite correctness of the work of Immanuel Velikovsky.

Well, its their funeral and its their loss. Its their choice of ignorance above wisdom, of sloth above industry and drowning before ship-building. Like Noah, it saddens me but there really isnt much I can do about it, short of beating them over the head with a rock book.

Ancient peoples made a number of photos, or photo-projection-paintings (or Rok-Fogo pictures) (in their language) of the coming down of the moon. Here is one.

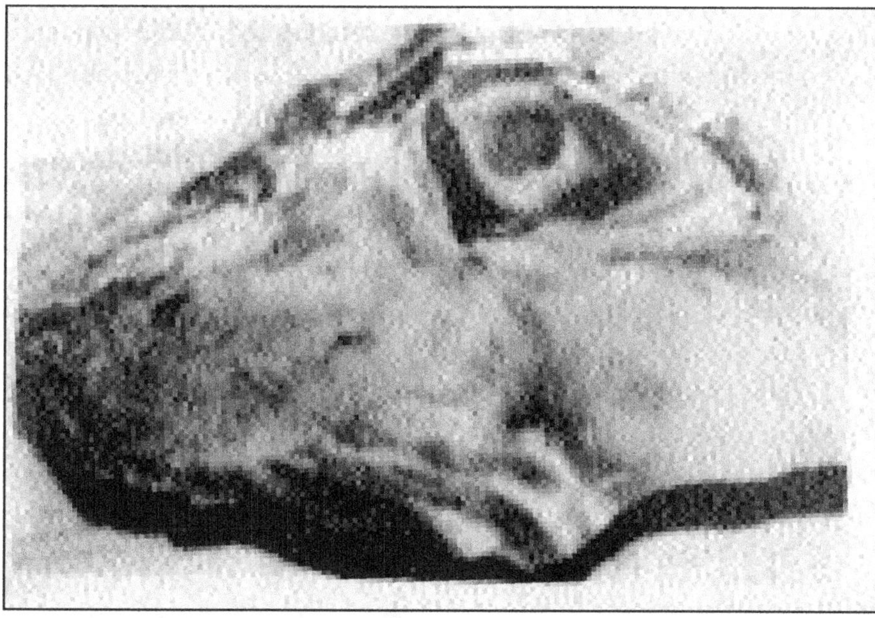

This was about all a lot of inhabitants saw of their own doom as it smashed down through the clouds and pulled their own oceans heaven high.

"The Fall" meant that the moon lost its own oceans, its own air and rocks and loose earth to the world when it bounced off and on.

On and up and out into a new orbit went the moon, but not the people and the beasts of Mother Earth. They lay dead and buried in the mud of their own ocean's bottoms where it had been pulled across the land, buried and smashed beneath the endless fall from the moon; the oceans and the air and the rocks and surface earth of the moon cane down in endless torrents of mud and water. The huge forests of earth were splintered into smashed piles of future coal and mud.

And the ancient cities of old earth, many of them built out of rock-books, were scattered over the world as a tidal wave rubble, pushed by the tidal wave movements round and round the earth under the falling moon.

The Mer-people of the oceans, lifted on high with their own ancient oceans and then smashed down into the mud and lava of the new-opened volcanoes... were dead and vanished forever from the world.

Science can say it never happened, but any curious child can find the rubble of old earth's cities, age-old in a tradition of true science. Little theater stones shaped like a concert shell, in which the warmth of the hand alone is enough to make the age-old pictures move again. Tiny book stones no bigger than a thimble, that once gave off magnificent color-pictures when placed in a projector. Huge boulder picture stones with life-sized human figures in them. Shoe-makers lasts that one could still make a shoe over. Stone type cast of liquids that hardened into the letters long ago. Flat stones once used for printing color-posters that will still print if inked. Buttons with little cast designs on them that long ago held their coats shut.

[Shaver stops the text at this point to include notes to his editor about photos. These notes continue for the rest of the manuscript's page and then picks back up with the main body of the text]

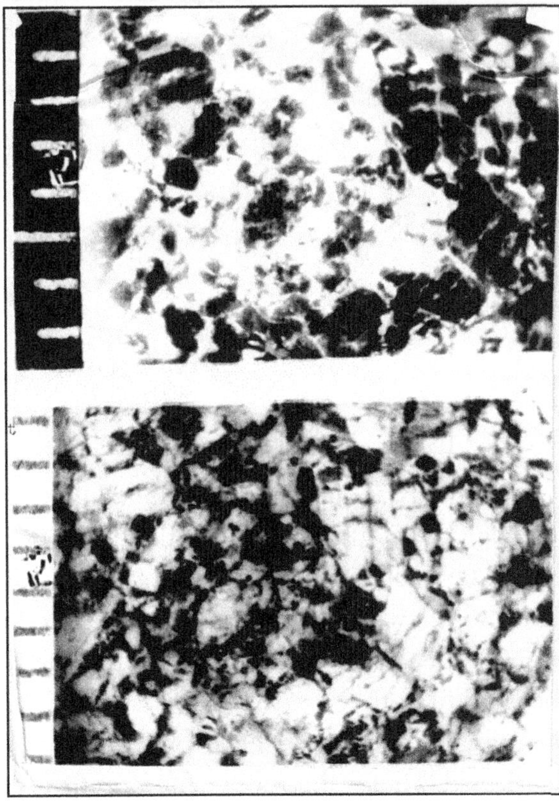

Speaks with forked tongue photo. Large profile covers height of print..all large pictures are made up of smaller. Every face of white has a black to contract it.. and vice versa.

Rap..if you think my prints are bad or obscure or puzzling look at a page full of Picasso prints they are far far more obscure and puzzling, and worse art by far... and whats more.. these are infinitely less childish in what message does get across.

One way to display these prints is to print a Picasso print of the kind (aren't theyall) and comment that Shaver rock photos are more intriguing and more thought provoking and even less puzzling by far

[Shaver continues with the main text]

isn't thinking correctly about such matters as mass, orbital velocity and spiral orbits.

Earth is just emerging from periods of time called the "Dark Ages". Science has itself a residue of dark ignorant dictums left over from those dark ages.

The cause of those ages of ignorance and of darkness is just overhead, shining down with its reflected light borrowed from the sun.

The moon was not always there. When the moon came, it plunged the earth into darkness, the darkness of death and destruction and world-wide blankets of mud and rubble, sand and gravel and the piled boulders of ancient cities so old even then no man knew their beginnings.

BUT we dont need to go on being ignorant victims of a wayward globe of rock. We dont have to submit to this world-wide ignorance of our own beginnings.

NOW we have the libraries left by the people of the pre-deluge world. They CAN be read.

They are encyclopedic, we can determine the exact number of scales on a mermaid's arm, the precise number of ribs in Adam's off-ox, if so inclined, just but a little expert work on the rock books.

But it will take more than one Shaver with his camera and saw. It will take teams of genuine scientists, rather than the wordy frauds we now accept as scientists.

It will take the kind of men and the wealth of equipment used in putting the Apollo crews on the moon.

And it will take the same kind of determination and decision and action.

It will take a little doing, in teams.

And so, leaving all that, lets think about the phrase "The Fall". The dark ages have left us a lot of singular documentation that indicates "The Fall" is a reference to the Fall of Satan and his Angels from (of all things) GRACE!

About the only real sense I can get out of all that documentation is that the probable name for the moon when it was a well known planet going round the sun was "Satan", a planet.

When the last of the rock books was written, after the fall had destroyed the ancient ways and most of the ancient original people, the phrase "The Fall" meant one thing alone. That thing was "The Fall of the Moon."

I gave you one of their depictions of the event, a photo of a slice of one of their rock books.

(Oddly enough, the other most planet of the solar system is named Pluto.)

According to modern descriptions of volcanic action during these world cataclysms, many new volcanoes were formed and all the old ones burst into new activity. The whole atmosphere of earth was permeated with sulphurous odors for centuries... and those are not my words, I will try to locate the quote for you.

But, in order to understand what seven separate moon-falls have done to earth, you had better read "Earth in Upheaval" by Velikovsky from cover to cover. No few quotes out of context can have the proper impact of the tremendous assembly of facts he gives.

Just why Velikovsky skirts the fact of moon-fALL I cant fathom, unless in truth he leans toward the reversal of the polarity of earth as a prime cause, or the shifting of the axis of earth as a prime cause.

Myself, I see the whole series of catastrophes which "Earth in Upheaval" substantiates and describes so successfully as results of moon-fall, and the reversal of polarity and the shift in the axis as results of impact with the moon.

To my mind, the unlikely poles of the moon magnet clicked together at impact, and the only reason we dont have them still stuck together is the same reversal as earth turned topsy turvy on impact. This threw the poles into LIKE positions of repellence, and the moon moved on into its new orbit because it was freed of the magnetic attraction.

But then I am only a layman, and such matters are really beyond me.

That the moon fell more than once is to me quite obvious, and when the digs reveal seven separate wide destructions I assume they were due to seven moon-falls.

I really dont need the moon to fall on me to take the hint, I get that feeling just by looking up at night.

The quotes and metionso of the many scientists as they discuss the ice ages and lava flows and dust clouds over centuries of time seem to me so much beating of a dead horse. Why cant they just look up and see that huge round accident waiting to happen again?

To my mind, and remember its a layman's mind, a scientific theory is some a scientist invents to keep from seeing the obvious and doing something about it, like real work.

For instance, about ten years ago I wrote to a very scientific gentleman, the Editor of Analog... about the rock book pictures, for some assistance in photographing and documenting their very obvious existence.

At that time I had neither a camera nor any lenses by ordinary reading glasses of the cheap four inch kind.

Her immediately went into the scientific theory stance and opined that since all such pictures were "accidentals" there wasn't any need for $50 a day.

Since I was broke as usual I didn't have a lot to say.

It is my theory that most scientific theories are like that... an easy wayout of a difficult job.

That is, too mnay scientists find it more practical to theorize than to ascertain the exact facts.

I remember one scientist explaining away a mammoth tooth I showed him by telling me that mammoths nor mastodons "had ever been found in Wisconsin".

It was almost exactly a week later that a steam shovel in Madison, the capital of Wisconsin, where he lived, uncovered a perfect mammoth skull. He would never have heard about that, I suppose, if some ignorant reporter hadn't put the photo into the Madison newspaper. I suppose the reporter hadn't heard about the scientist.

To this poor layman, all scientists who puzzle and puzzle through endless volumes of stilted prose about the mysterious causes of earths so obvious and so numerous world wide cataclysms are typical scientists, who cant see the forest because they are studying a tree.

To me, the nearest and most obvious cause is the first one to examine. And I really cannot understand why they have all been so busy puzzling over the causes of world wide cataclysm with the moon sailing overhead.

But then I am a man who spent nearly fifteen years trying to get one scientist to look at just one rock, really look, without the slightest success.

Everyone of them came up with an excuse to avoid getting out a microscope or a magnifier, the while he labeled his voluminous excuses for not doing anything at all with the very scientific term...his theory!

Personally I will take a bricklayer any day. At least he knows that if a brick falls on your head, it hurts.

Now you know why this book is called "The Layman's Atlantis". That means it is for people who can have a cause and an effect without demanding a theory.

I once sent an artifact bearing very interesting and artistic designs on it to the Smithsonian. They wrote me a letter asking for 55 cents to ship back my "boulder". Now even I knew a rock that small is not a boulder.

I sent the same rock to a photo-curio shop in New York to photograph the ancient per-ice-age art on it. They did so, and sent me my very first B&W slides of per-deluge art, very interesting to me. I subsequently sold that same rock to a fan of mine for $25 as an artifact. But, to the Smithsonian it was a boulder, bare of all significance. I have had my own suspicions about all scientists ever since.

Personally I actually think they didnt know the difference between a boulder and a small rock, in fact, and didn't actually mean to cast aspersions on my artifact.

There is in fact a blind spot in all over-educated people, I have learned. They have an opinion a man is less intelligent if he hasn't spent most of his live in a school.

My own opinion about that is that a man who has been helped to walk all his life doesn't know how to walk alone.

But there you have an opinion that is like all opinions, a substitute for the real facts. It was real scientists who put the Apollo into orbit around the moon. They weren't working with theories or opinions.

Now if I could just get one of my boulders into their hands, they might find out it was a rock more worthwhile than the ones they brought from the moon. Its my opinion we have endless tons of moon rocks already, that fell when the whole surface of the moon fell on earth...the first moon-fall, that is.

Now to show them a moon-rock from the sands of Wisconsin is the problem, for me as insuperable as the first flight to the moon seemed back when they started the Apollo project. It seems my moon-rocks are boulders. But I am only a layman.

One day I will meet a real scientist and I will find it is possible to tell them about moon-rocks already on earth for a long, long time. Or will they have a theory to keep from bending over and picking up one of those so heavy boulders?

But then, right now I'm writing instead of putting my new microscope adapter on my microscope so I can take some pictures. Maybe they have to write books to make a living is why they cant get any real work done.

While I didn't start out to emphasize the moon-fall theory over any other aspect of the fate of the Elder World, it is crucial. Mainly its crucial because its what happened, and I dont know how to tell it as if it might have happened some other way just to please some people.

Velikovsky in the final pages of "Earth in Upheaval" draws a picture of the old astronomy as a theoretical picture of the celestial mechanism "wound up to go on forever". He states that "this picture is based upon a mechanistic view of the universe which considers magnetism not at all!"

He goes on to explain that sun observers have noted that solar prominences repel each other actively (something I predicted 25 years ago in science-fiction writings) and that many another phenomenon in astronomical work can only be studied and understood by including magnetic forces and polarities...ect.

All of which he adds up to mean that astronomy is fallible and makes very grave errors that can only be explained by unincluded magnetic forces which are nevertheless active and powerful in spite of the ignoring attitude of "Astronomy".

Bravo to Velikovsky, he actually said it!

But I want to point out that the moon is in stable orbit only because the poles parallel earth's poles at present. What would happen if the poles of the moon drifted so that one attracted one more than the other... or vice versa? Unlikes attract and likes repel doesn't really require solar flare observation to notice, does it?

Velikovsky's concept of earth cataclysms caused by the advent of passing comet would only need to shift the attitude of the moon enough to point one pole toward earth more than it does now, to have extremely powerful forces come into play.

The point I want to make is that the moon's orbital stability actually depends upon quite other forces than only gravity and velocity in orbit.

In Velikovsky's analyses he has the series of catastrophes caused by the entry of a large comet.

To my mind you dont need a comet's entry to have the catastrophes inevitable and frequent. You only need a moon that lets it magnetic poles drift into alignment with earth's in such a way that likes repel and unlikes attract forcibly enough to cause further drift and further magnetic forces to result...etc.

In other words moon's attitude to-earth's poles is most probably the determing factor in moon's orbital deviations in the past and will be the cause of orbital failure in the future as well.

Why Velikovsky skirts this obvious cause of moon-falls as well as the moon-falls in his writings I cannot fathom unless he has such a hearty respect for the venom and non -co-operation of offended scientists that he simply cannot state the meanings of the observed catastrophes... its too much for me.

To me its obvious that astronomy has mastered the art of the sin of omission in ignoring the moon as well as the biblical deluge and the seven cultures of earth in the past that were destroyed by the moon-falls.

To me Fort has the whole astronomical world fairly well analyzed in his chapters on astronomy. What Fort would have to say with one of my rock books in his hands I would like to hear.

Moon-rocks as well as the artifacts of seven dead cultures litter the hills and morainen and cut-banks of half the world... and we send a rocket to the moon to get a moon-rock.

My feelings are really that "science" is the art of non-observation!

The presence of unobserved rock books in nearly every rock pile on earth leads me to believe they will always manage to make mistakes in preference to doing some actual observational work in ascertaining the truth about anything.

So, if you want to feel safe under that gibbous moon you read some old astronomy books which place everything in the sky held there by very well balanced forces.

But if you want to know what happened to the vanished cultures whose books are available to anyone who looks for them on almost any hillside... you read Velikovsky with the mental reservation that he was at great pains not to offend the great cult of "science: and didn't quite make it, anyway.

I once asked a curator of a large municipal museum why he hung certain copies as genuine, and he told me that he couldn't afford to offend the people who had presented them.

If you read Velikovsky carefully you cant help but visualize some very dignified idiots.

With the moon hanging overhead every night I feel we should offend someone.

It could matter, weightily

***

THIS IS A PAINTING MADE BY PROJECTING A SLICE OF A ROCK BOOK ON TO A SENSITIZED CANVAS. THEN I PAINT COLOR ON THE PICTURE. I PUT IT HERE TO ACQUAINT YOU WITH THE STYLE OF ART,& THE HUMOR IN THE PICTURES THAT FILL ROCK BOOKS.

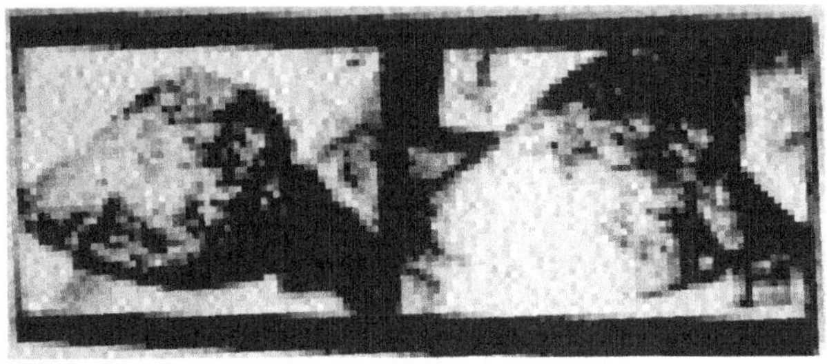

CHAPTER

Speaking of rocks

did you really ever look at one? They are covered with the most marvelous raised pictorials!

What's more, the pictures go all the way through the rock! Impossible, but true.

The really weird thing about rock book, after I knew something about them from several years of study of them, was NOT their contents.

The really weird thing about rocks in the fact that the whole population of this old earth has managed to ignore them!

How did they manage this piece of tomfoolery?

But a little library research reassured me. It seems that as late as 1700 sailors took gazing stones to sea with them to pass the time in the forecastle!

And that not much earlier the last of the troubadours was still singing from stones he carried with him!

And that not much earlier than that gazing stones were an article of commerce. So the total population of earth has not been entirely blind, always.

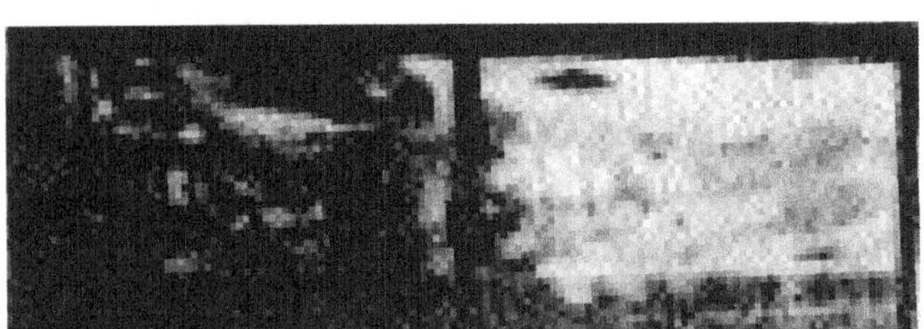

This is the "rock" from which the monster on opposite page was enlarged. You can find him in the left center.

To get the most out of these complex montages of monsters, mermaids, and other lively and ungentle creatures of the far past... you must learn to tilt and turn your rock slowly to let the light outline each face and figure... for that is how they were made to be seen. This is not a difficult skill, but it does have to be learned.

You had better learn to collect these for yourself while they are still available on mountain slopes and dry river beds... for civilization has a way of destroying all traces of the past... just as the strip mines are destroying the lovely mountains of Kentucky.

One day these despised "rocks" will bring prices no diamond ever did... for they have a vast value beyond all the superficial glitter of any diamond.

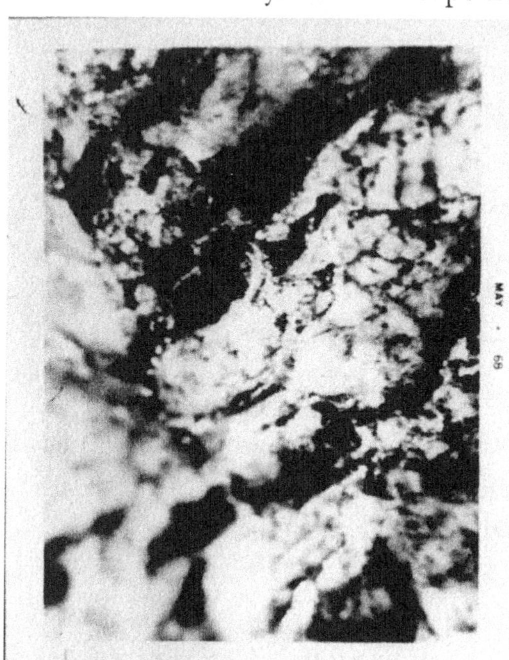

This monster's head is one of a great many on this rock, which is shown at left. If you look just left of center on the rock, you find the reptilian head of which this is an enlargement.

This whole rock is a montage of brawling reptilian head of several varieties. If you are interested in the age of dinosaurs as it really was, and not as it is sometimes misrepresented in mistaken textbooks, then you can see it for yourself in such rocks as this.

TO ME, THE FACE ABOVE IS PLAINER

than the photo of myself, below, holding the rock from which the photo above was taken.

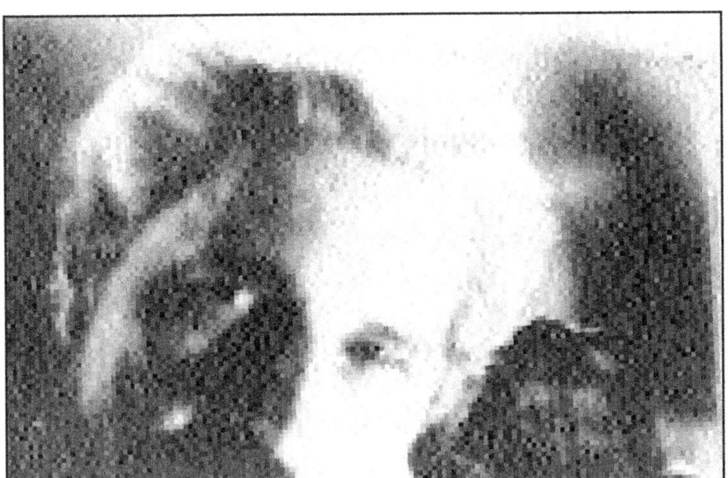

That rock is the most valuable object in our world, and its kind are totally ignored by our so-wonderful science that put a man on the moon and brought back fifty pounds of moon rocks. I wonder if they will manage to ignore all the images in the rocks from the moon, too?

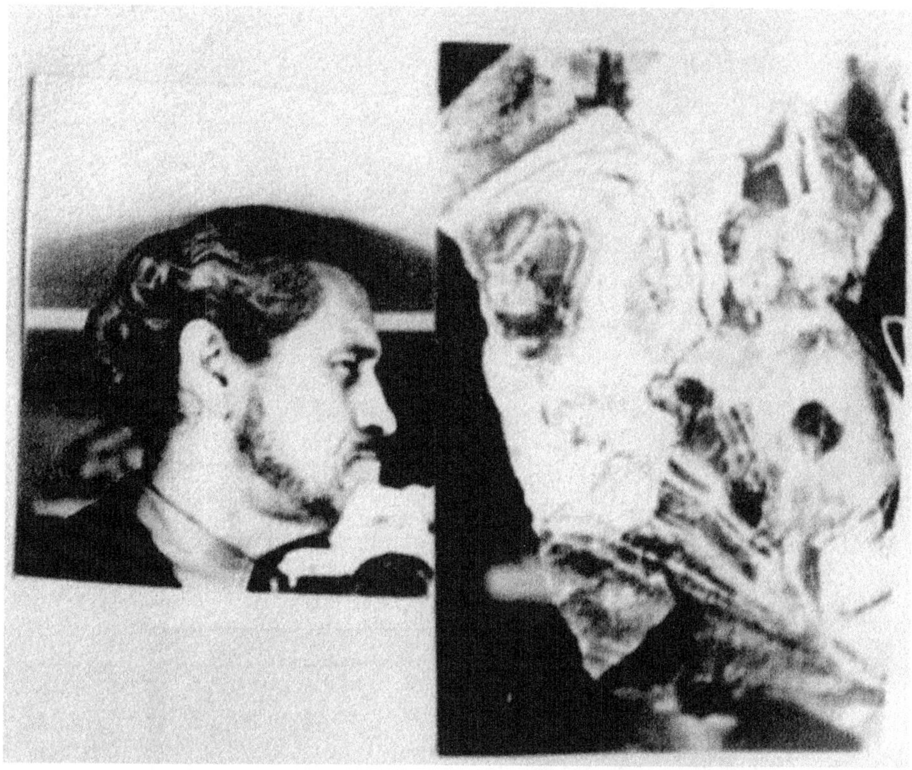

There is a man's profile in the rock photo on the right. I juxtaposed my own profile because I am a ham and because I want to show that the ancient great races resembled us... were in fact our ancestors.

We are the sons of Gods in truth. Once before the moon fell our kind multiplied through all space...and our relatives are out there, awaiting is.

Why dont we know this?

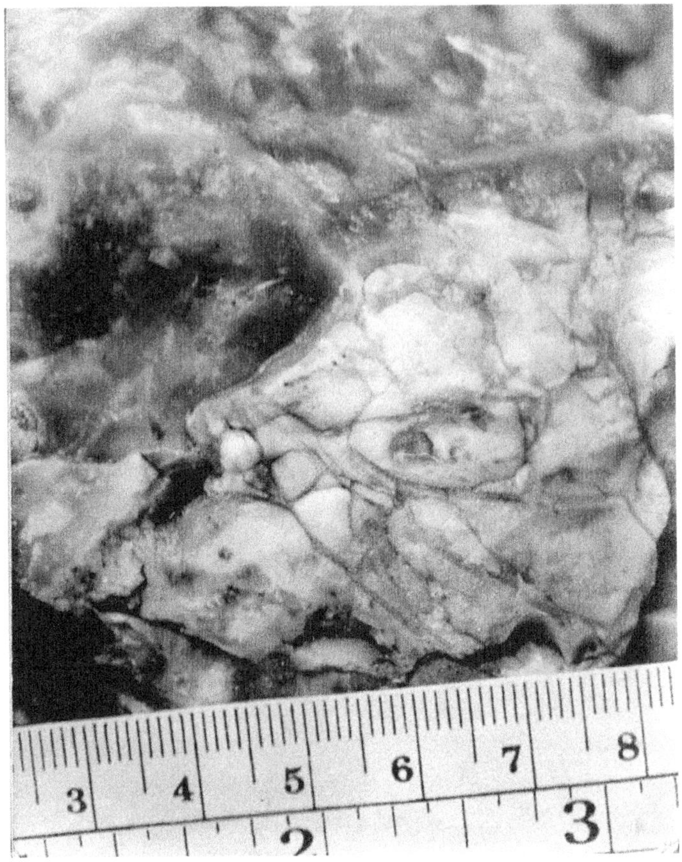
3 4 5 6 7 8
2 3

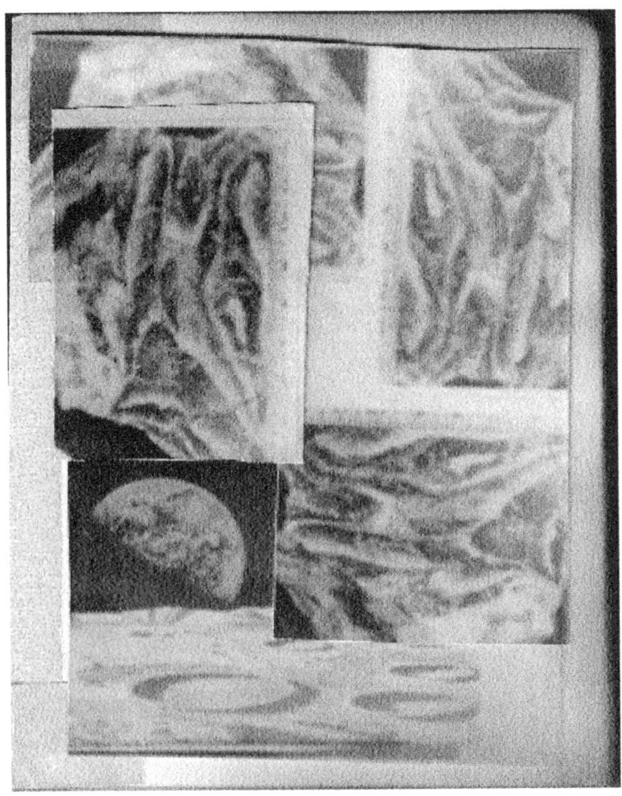

ON ROGFOGOS

Laying a lens on the projection under an enlarger draws a white circle around the part you want to emphasize and sharpens the image slightly. Tinting portions gives a better contrast to the face you want... if you look at the duplicate print in B&W you can see the original before tinting.

Such faces in sliced book rock are amazing compound images made up up of a number of smaller images, this system of putting many images into a very small space had an endless long time of development to reach the efficiency it has.

These people are often wearing spectacles. The academic look of them is no accident, they were very bookish people. The faces themselves are a form of writing now lost, I suspect, because of the Mayan system of writing with faces in rows which survived into comparatively recent times.

Looking at such pictures one has to constantly remind one-self of their immense age, these rock books contents are as old as the image of the man in the moon. Think how long ago that picture was placed on the moon, to appreciate the length of corroding time that has passed over and faded the images in these rock books.

HAVE YOU EVER REALLY TAKEN A GOOD LOOK?

HOW TO SHOOT ROCK BOOKS BY RICHARD S. SHAVER

From *Psychic Observer*, Feb.-March, 1973

Coming face to face with the facts of rock books, new viewers are apt to envision all sorts of difficulties which do not really exist. Rock books contain engraved surfaces with engravings quite as plain as any minted coin - if you look for them. There is only real difficulty. People don't like to work. And it is work to paw over piles of potato-sized rocks in search of the elusive single best example.

However, in the process of pawing they forget to really look. Rock books are very numerous in any rock pile of surface rock (as opposed to rocks of alluvial origin smashed up by machinery)

- Richard S. Shaver

People expect rock books to give perfect pictures first crack with the camera. They do, in fact, do just that... But the art is so complex that it is not readily recognized as art.

As you cut a plane through a rock book you cross section the original 3-dimensional organization of picture planes and get a complex montage of see-through pictorials and parts of human figures that is endlessly confusing. But so is a photo of Rubens painting taken from two inches away confusing. It's nothing but a couple of brush marks. So is a photo of a pointillist painting confusing, taken at six inches. It is nothing but dots.

When your camera does in fact coincide the original scan frames of a rock book (from 2 to 4 mm rectangles) then you loose a lot of confusion and get a sensible picture. But since all pictures are really aerial images you do have to get the focal lengths just right.

Very few people have genuinely correct concepts of optical facts and art facts in their minds...so that the difficulties in explaining the facts about rock books are endlessly complicated by the lack of facts about optics in minds of the bearers.

They simply cannot grasp what you are talking about when you say, "To see rock book pictures you must allow for variant focal lengths and strobe type see-thoughts and over prints and transparent places, etc"

So one fails to explain simply the simple facts about rock books because the complexities of educating the average person to all the many angles of optics is just too much.

Optics is a science much neglected by our school systems.

All that I ever learned about optics I learned by trial and error and by fishing through all sorts of books for them. I didn't learn it in school.

For instance...the moon contains perfect examples of rock art in huge size. The man in the moon is well known to most people, but how many of them ever recognized the picture in the moon as a man-made picture rather than an accidental one?

The moon contains many pictures other than the man in the moon, and they all show up quite well at certain angles in photos or are swallowed up in the marks of the meteor craters in others. It all depends on the chiaroscuro sought...the kind of contrast looked for and achieved...and the angle from which the astronaut took the pictures, etc., etc.,

Here is a moon photo purposely blurred to achieve an all-over pictorial look rather than just a lot of high contrast pock marks. Note there is a needle-nosed female wearing a tiara who may or may not be an accidental apparition. Truth is, she is not...but I don't want to argue the point. (Illustration 1)

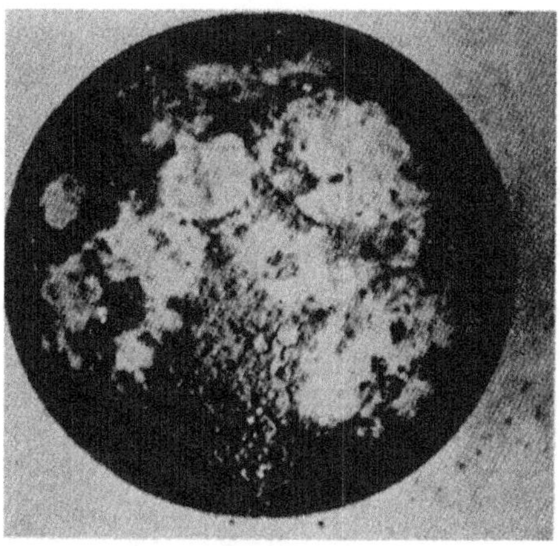

No. 2

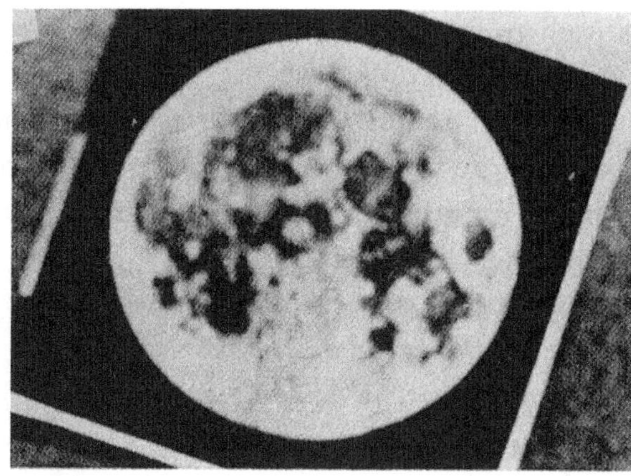

No. 1

Reversing the black and white and turning the negative over, left to right produces a photo in which the needle-nosed woman disappears, to be replaced by a man shouting and holding his nose...which is symbolic of who knows what at this late date. (Illustr. No. 2)

In case, you do not really have to LOOK for rock book images to see what they look like, they sail over head every night and they are also seen every day on "Today" when the continent of Africa comes on the background behind Barbara. The African continent plus Europe plus Asia make together a very fair bust of Aphrodite...giving rise to the speculation..."Did God indeed when he created the earth have a crush on Aphrodite?"

With England serving as the frontispiece on Aphrodite's helmet and all of Asia forming her flying hair...one wonders about the story of God Creating earth...or maybe it was Aphrodite?

In any case there peculiarly outstanding examples of ancient races' predilection fro decorating things like planets do lend a hand to the orthodox religionists' constant repetition of the phrase..."God created the earth" because He sure left a lot of His drawing on it.

Actually, the ancient great races use of planets for footstools and space buoys on which they pained their space beacon symbols to give them the speed and direction and size of the planet without having to compute it all every time they passed...has left us some outstanding examples of the space people's handiwork.

They made such projections upon planets and moons and other bodies with great "integrative force rays which cause a raised design on anything they strike". And they used the same sort of ray forces to engrave rock book and to put the images inside the rock books for you to read.

That the original great space races colonized earth is plain enough (or anyone to see if they look for their handiwork. It is everywhere one looks. But one does have to look with an open mind and an eye that can accept some slight deterioration as natural in anything so old.

For me to take on the phalanxes God-shouters and try to explain that rock books are really more omnipresent even that Gideon Bibles and much more important in content...is for me to say truth and them to misunderstand the truth as usual.

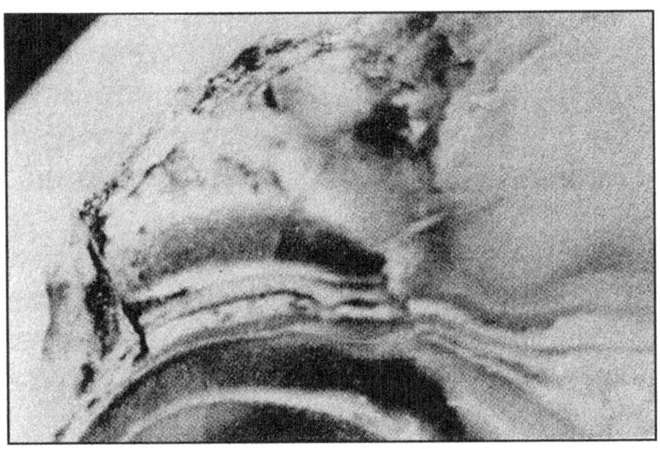

But I don't really crave for the privilege because they all have a much louder voice than I. Like truth, I have only a still small voice and a moon and a planet or two to back me up.

But I do have reason and vision on my side, if they insist upon arguing.

For instance, you can make any number of portraits of space men in their space gear...and all of them will be better looking than this example of a space trader. For the Amazons with whom he is discussing trade were quite scornful of him and his appearance and what he had to offer them. What is important is not he is a Hitler-like character full of bombast...but his space gear and what we can learn from it.

Note, his collar is quite tight and is stuffed with paddling to keep his head from moving during acceleration and take-off. There is a metal neck brace at the back of the collar as further insurance against whip lash movement of the head. There is a little black hand symbol a the back pointing out the hinge detail that attaches his helmet to the neck brace metal. He couldn't lose or remove that helmet... it was always ready and in place to make a seal when closed...the rock books tell it like it was.

ANCIENT HISTORY IN STONE

From *SEARCH*, July, 1973

([Search Magazine]Editor's note: *This article is abstracted from the forthcoming book by Richard S. Shaver THIS ANCIENT EARTH-ITS STORY IN STONE, now in production. We believe you will find it fascinating and provocative. But it can only begin to suggest the incredible discovery that is set forth in this book, perhaps the most important writings of this controversial figure, who has already become a legend among his millions of followers. And now, modern electronics science is beginning to duplicate (and corroborate) an ancient science, as it is reveled here in Shaver's discovery of an incredible "library in stone" left scattered over the Earth by the ravages of the ancient "Deluge" of the Bible)*

It all began, for me, when my wife came in from the field with several "pretty stones" and said: "Richard, there are pictures on these stones!" I was amused at first, but when she showed me the stones, and I saw what she had seen- and more! - I went stone-hunting myself, and began a 25-year study of what I have come to call "rock books". I am convinced that is what they are, and in this article, I intend to give you a glimpse into the ancient past. It is said that seeing is believing. I don't ask you to believe! I ask you to look for yourself! The rock-book stones lie everywhere, and you can find your own; and with a little patience and a little serious examination and study, you can see for yourself!

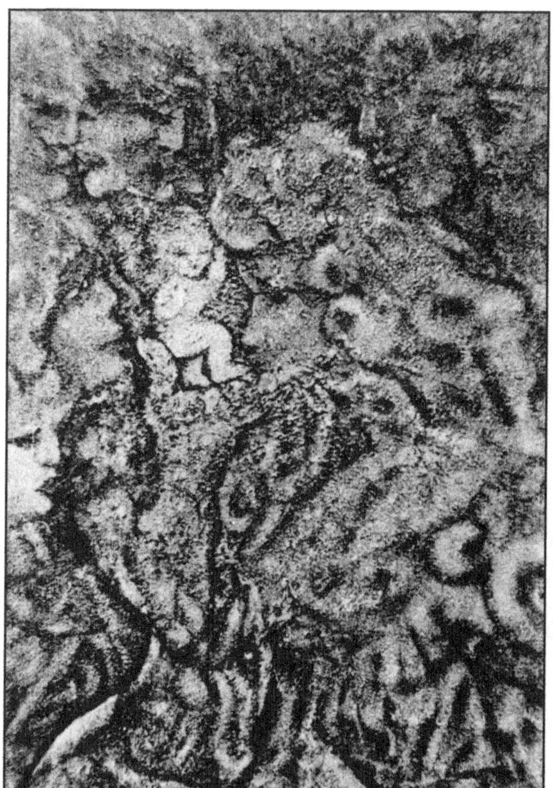

This (and other) "paintings" presented in this article were made by putting a slice of rock in an overhead projector and projecting it on a wet canvas. At the same time powdered marine glue is sifted into the light of the projection, which pushes the falling flue into a raised line image or emboss pattern of the light and dark portions of the projected image. These raised images are then "developed" by dragging a dry brush (one way only) across the ridges to emphasize the pattern. Another method is to coat the canvas with photo-sensitive material and project the image of the rock with the opaque projector.

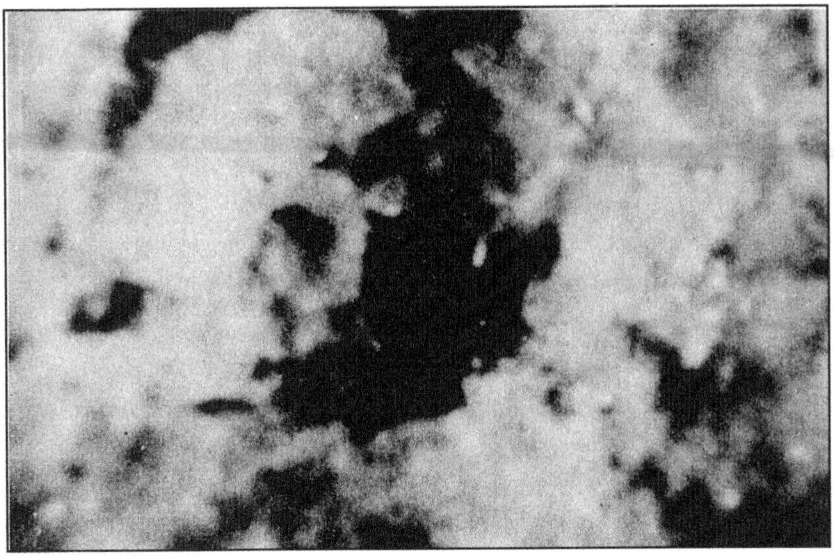

This actual highly magnified photo of a rick slice can be viewed from all four angles. The dark area in the center is the significant area to study here. It is a reversible face and also a composite face. Note the white face facing the dark area, and then the front view of another face composed of both light and dark areas. See if you can find the several female profiles and a fierce male face. Due to the angle of the cut, all faces are slightly out of focus.

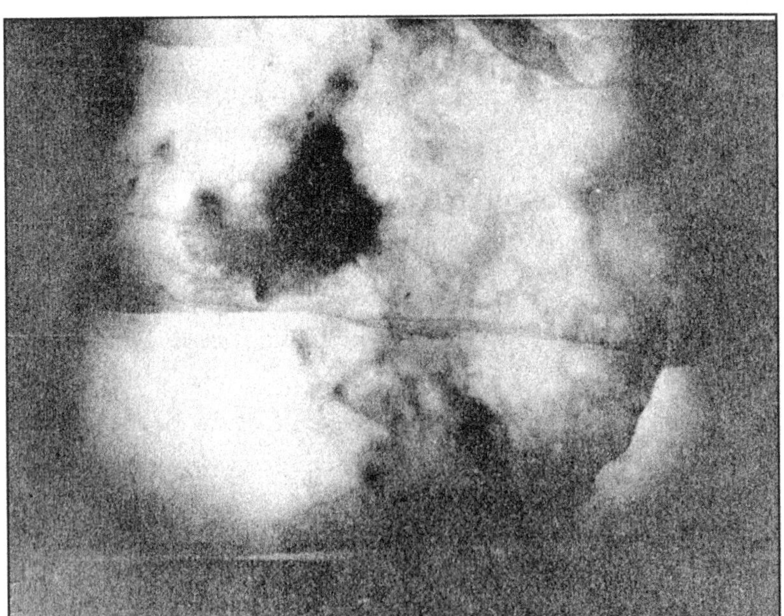

Another slice of stone photographed with light shining through it from the back side. The face on the right is male, wearing a round helmet, and its owner is apparently embracing the female facing him on the left. Directly between their faces can be seen a front view of a small child, probably symbolic of their union.

It seems to me that Earth is far older than any of our scientists estimate and far different in its life content from anything they try to explain.

If planets start as specks of dust in space, and grow by slow acquisition of space-dust into marbles, and the marbles gradually into something like planetoids...then after a long, long time of slow growing, they are caught by the whirling gravitational field of some larger body and become satellites.

If you accept this view of the beginning of Earth, then you can perhaps see that on such a small ball caught by the whirling magnetic gravity of a sun into new movement in a vast circle...conditions would become very different because of the new and sudden warmth.

The age of slow acquisitive growth of space-dust is the age of Earth, really. You cannot say it figures. You have to visualize the immense span of time, so much greater than imagination can envision.

To understand this, think of gravity as a "something". Just because you cannot see it, doesn't mean it isn't a "something". It is a very "powerful something" that flows steadily into the earth and remains there. And it remains because it becomes something else-matter, rock, what-will-you-it becomes earth!

Gravity is itself the growth of earth-matter going on and on. It is a "real something", and it makes Earth grow. I think gravity as the roots of a plant and that plant is Earth - the planet. It certainly is not a spirit force, real but unreal.

To grasp the concept of early life on Earth you have to see it as a marble in size, caught up by a giant sun long ago. It swung about the sun, and it was a living planet, warmed by the distant huge sun. It had air, because planets live and air is part of their life. Water condensed in the air and became oceans.

In these oceans life began to move, Earth had life, and I think of such life on a planet as necessary part of its life, just as in your body the blood-cells are a necessary part of your life.

That is what people and fish and animals and oysters, etc.etc., really are! They are the blood-cells, the working parts of an immense life form...the planet.

A planet is alive, and its people are its blood-cells, circulating in its seas, moving over its land. When we are healthy and the life is normal, then we know what to do, just as our blood-cells know what to do, and they carry carbon dioxide away and bring the fresh oxygen, and so on and so on. Nobody tells them-they know. It is that knowing that is really built in to life. Like gravity, you can't see it. We call it the sense of right and wrong, or we call it conscience, or we do not have any and call it nonsense. In the latter case, we are abnormal blood-calls of the plant planet...sick and burdensome to our greater life-mother Earth.

The "projector" painting shows a confused mass of intermingled large and small figures and faces of the difficulty of matching the focal length of the original images with that of the projector, and the :accidental" angle of the "cut" of the stone. Thus the projector throws out all these images simultaneously. Note the many tiny images of the hair, the many instances of composite images (different angles of the same face in the same image)

This is a "four-way" picture rock. But when using a one-way movement of the dry brush, the other three embosses are usually obscured or eliminated. However, two images usually come out anyway, one of them "upside down", or in reverse black

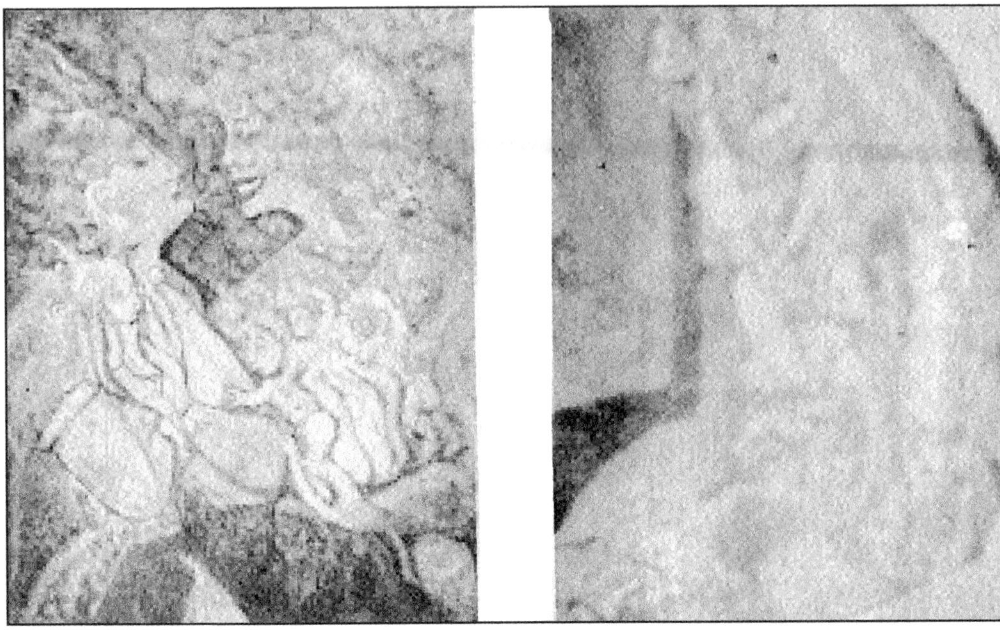

In these two photos, one of the projected painting, the other of a slice of very hard agate, we see the images quite plainly in both, even though they are probably separated in time by perhaps hundreds of thousands of years, because the stones vary greatly in geological age.

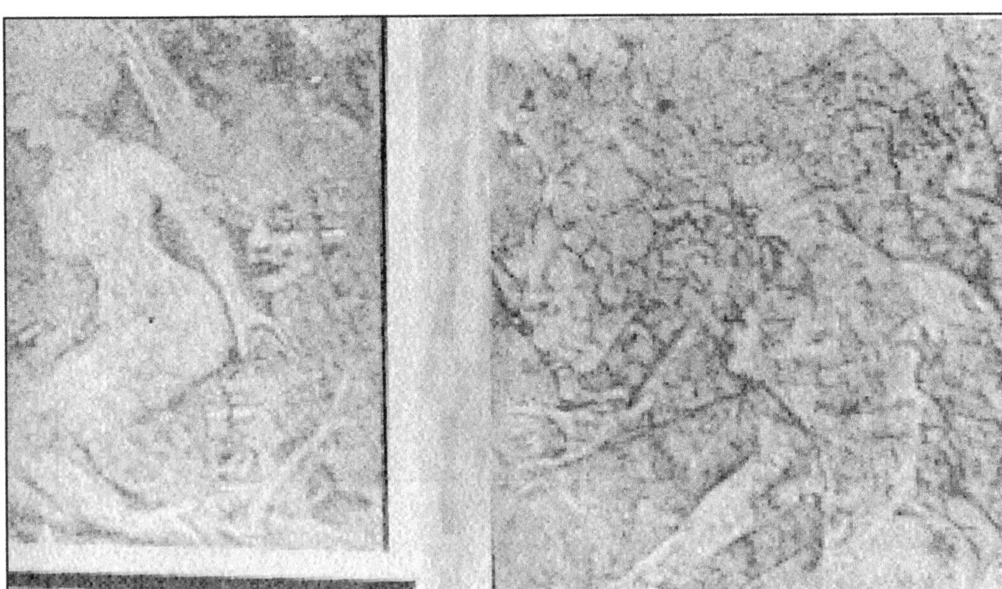

These two rock paintings seem quite obvious-they are scenes of marriages. Marriages are always fun-the bride is being carried aloft, either on a shoulder, or on a special carrying chair. Note the immense confusion and profusion of tiny images (due to the plane of the cut being at the wrong angle) in the painting on the right.

To me, this is all built-in inherited knowledge. No one taught me. I just know it.

No one had to teach that early life on the planet Earth what to do or how to do it. It knew, and it did what the mother earth needed. It was healthy and good and not ignorant; It had the mother's vast ancient wisdom built-in when it was born!

Church people call built-in sensitivity to the greater life above us "soul", or they call it "divine knowledge", or they burden it all down with mystic references in large and nonunderstandable words of no real content.

But we commoners and laymen do not need telling, or teaching, or large and ponderous words thrown at us from every side. We know...we were born with the mother's umbilical cord still tight fast to our minds...and we know what she needs us.

So don't blame us if we feel scornful of those with no sting attached, They are orphans, and we don't know why they are orphans or why they don't know.

So when I talk about "This Ancient Earth", it is of a dying mother speaking to her children, exhorting them to find a way of their own, now that they have finally slain her with their misbehavior.

Our Mother Earth is not old as planets go, perhaps, but she has been moving through some terrible times, and the dead moon has struck her too many blows for everything to be quite right with her health.

We haven't been good children for a long time now, but she knows why. I often think she has been unconscious or things would be different. But one can't know if that is true or not, or if she feels the pain of wrongfulness or not.

Anyway, this article is about the ancient times of Earth's youth, when people were much larger of body and longer of life. Then the seas were not salt, and the air was not soiled with industry and its chimneys and its motor cars. Air was quite invigorating, and life was long and happy and filled with a sense of accomplishment and rightness that is no longer present.

From the rock records we can draw a picture of the whole of the past eras of Earth's history under the domination of mankind. They can only show you the world as it was during a high state of civilization. For when the rock books were made, long, long ago, people had learned the immensely complex optical science behind the pictures in the rock books. (Just as we are now impressing millions of pictures and information on cubes of crystal with laser beams.)

But oddly enough one can find rock books of a very simple, childlike kind. Were they made first, during an age of slow development of the mind and science. It seems not. They could be the product of children in school, learning how.

One hesitates, because of our present day shibboleths and fixations to say what the truth about the beginnings really may be.

Yet to me it occurs again and again that the true beginnings of mankind are dual. There was life on Earth, and there was life on other planets...and somewhere along the line of time and travel and the infinitudes of space the line of mankind's origin gets hidden. I can't say for sure mankind did NOT begin on Earth. I can't say for sure man did not being on Earth and develop from scratch the sciences of space vessels.

We may never be sure. But it looks to me as though man may be a true son of Earth and Earth's oceans and no hybrid of space races. For the Mers of our oceans do indeed go back to the very beginnings of Earth itself.

"The Merm", as they called themselves, are the only genuine authorities about the earliest world, which was a world of water, mostly.

There were the Manoarfin, the Khmer, the Merfin, the Finns, etc,. but generally speaking they were called the Merm.

The Merm have come down to us only in our legends of the Mermaids. The male mermen are hardly ever mentioned in legends.

Like varying species of fish they have their differences. In some, the males are larger than the females, and vice versa. One notices that some pictures of Mers show a very large female compared to the small male.

The scientists who look for a missing link among landlubber species are so wide of the mark it is laughable. They have been looking for the "link" in a tree for a good long time now. Mermen were not very expert at climbing trees!

The merm were very bookish, and they made so many of them one knows they were as numerous as ay other fish in those early oceans. Pondering on the vast numbers of rock books, one only begins to understand it when one thinks, "What would New York be like if newspapers would not burn?"

It would be buried under its own newsprint! They wouldn't survive very many Sundays of some of those big Sunday editions.

The Merm made very durable "newspaper" rock books and they saved all of them for they were a practical people. They even built houses out of them!

When I first found the rock books I had no intention of doing anything like work with them. I thought all I had to do was tell about them, and others would go to work on them and tell me all about them.

It was then I found that present-day American science was not receptive to being informed of the presence of rock books in the farmer's rock piles. They couldn't be told. It was like trying to wake the dead, or get the President on the phone, or like a postman trying to get a raise.

Mer book-rock were shaped to be put together. There are little ledges and keys so that properly fitted they make their own shelves, and will stack in a certain shape. That is, a stack of Mer rock originally was formed to fit together in a figure, a sculpture of some significant shape. these most ancient of all libraries were so stacked so, under water, like so many sculptures arranged in the Mer idea of order.

Other rocks were shaped as they are to fit into the projector axle. The projector had a shaft with a socket into which the rock fitted, and turned slowly, the pickup eyes of the device scanned in a certain spiral sequence.

All this forgotten gadgetry of the forgotten peoples will have to be recreated from the rock-book pictures if we are ever to read them properly.

This is a new field, a new science. I started it. There are few quotes because there are no others to quote. There are so experts in pre-deluge artifacts; so far as I know I am the only one who ever really looked at any rock respectfully.

The optics of rock books are tricky. They need study to be appreciated. But, in spite of that, one can with almost no help but a couple of reading glasses over each other get a great deal out of any rock book.

It is that great deal I have to give you--a simple man's first look at a heretofore hidden past. The first man of our line, the "missing link" between man's evolution and the beast world, has been sought by antiquarians all over the world. And all that time he was starting at them form the rocks they ignored.

A battle scene between an Amazon and a giant ape-bat. With an ape's terrific strength, coupled with a bat's dive bomber technique, they were apt to bowl you off your feet and have your throat wide open before you knew what hit you. This picture was made by projecting the stone slice with an opaque projector onto a canvas doped with photo-sensitive chemicals.

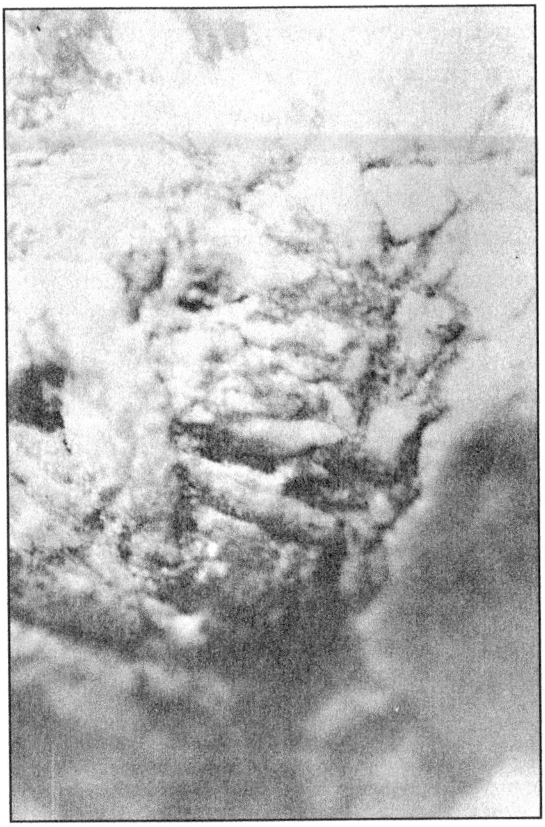

A direct photo from a rock itself-showing a close-up portrait of the ape-bat depicted in the preceding battle scene.

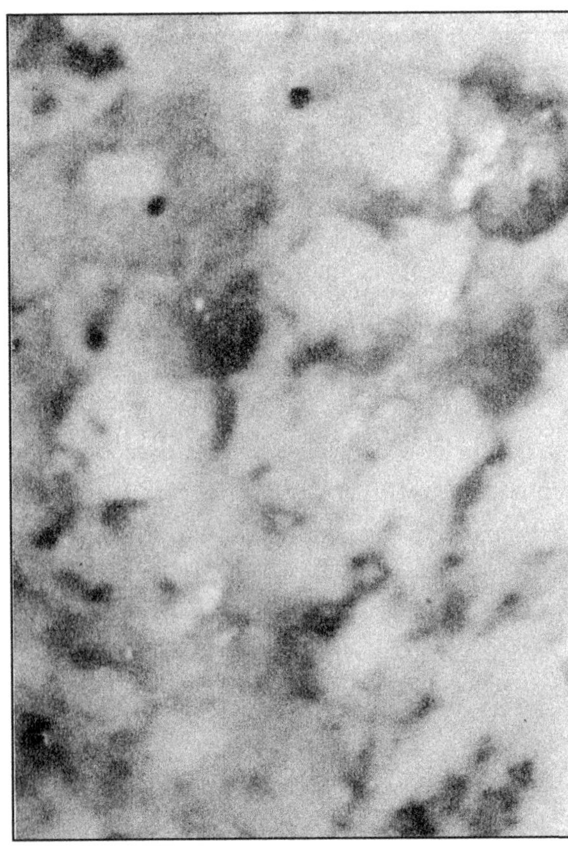

Photo of the sawed face of a rock sent from Viet Nam. Such faces as these run all the way through the rocks, and to call them accidental is to ignore the illogic of a rock crammed with faces. Today we "photograph" thousands of pictures by means of laser beams in one crystal cube smaller than a sugar cube. What we need is a better scientific way of bringing out the photos in these ancient crystalline stones.

Here are two actual photos of the same stone. One of them is focused on the plane surface of the stone, showing the many partial pictures the saw passed through. Visible also are the saw-marks. The confusion is evident, yet the picture can be seen by study. By focusing on just one of the faces in the semi-transparent stone, we get the picture on the top. This is done by deliberately diffusing hte focus so as to reduce distracting details. Each photo in these rocks has its own view-lane, and one is clearer than the other because the saw passed closer to this view-plane.

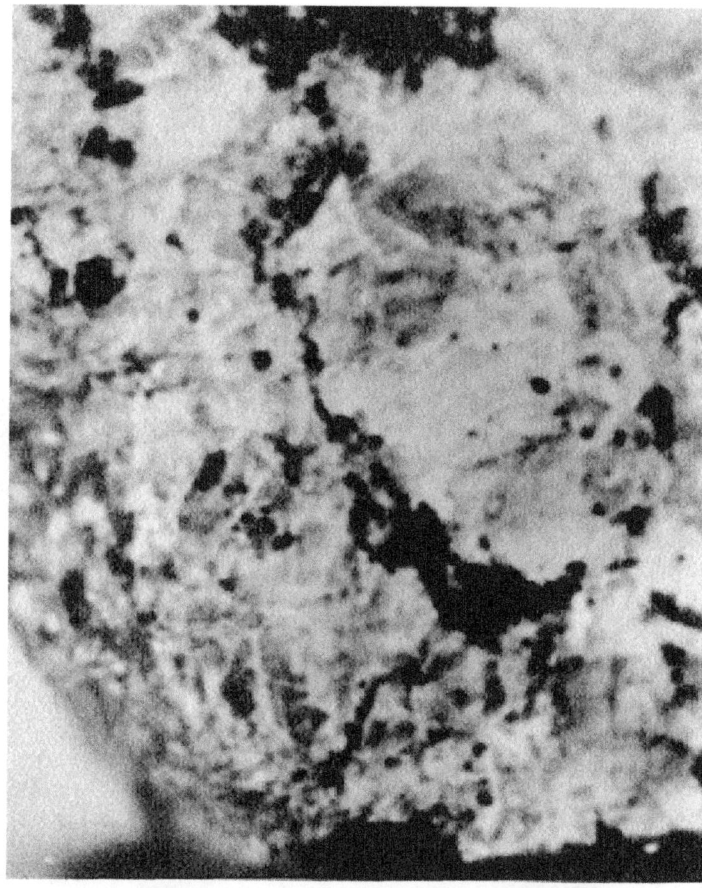

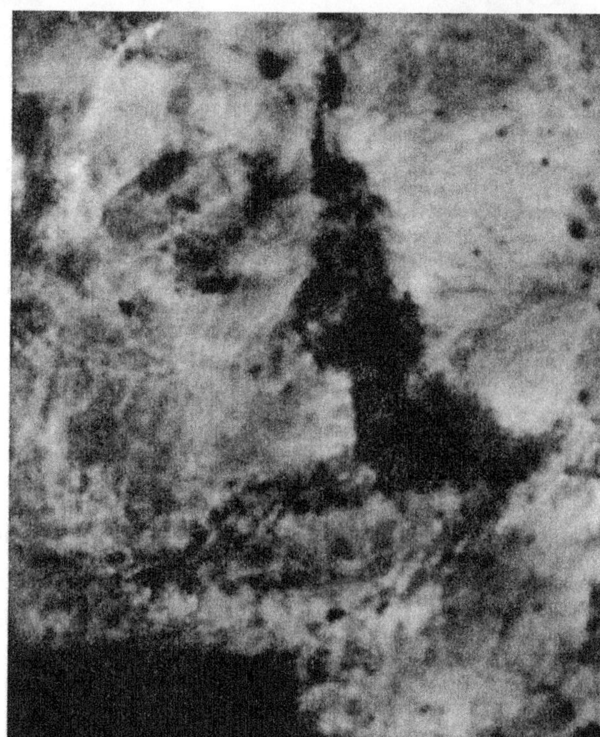

ROGFOGO: PICTURES IN STONE

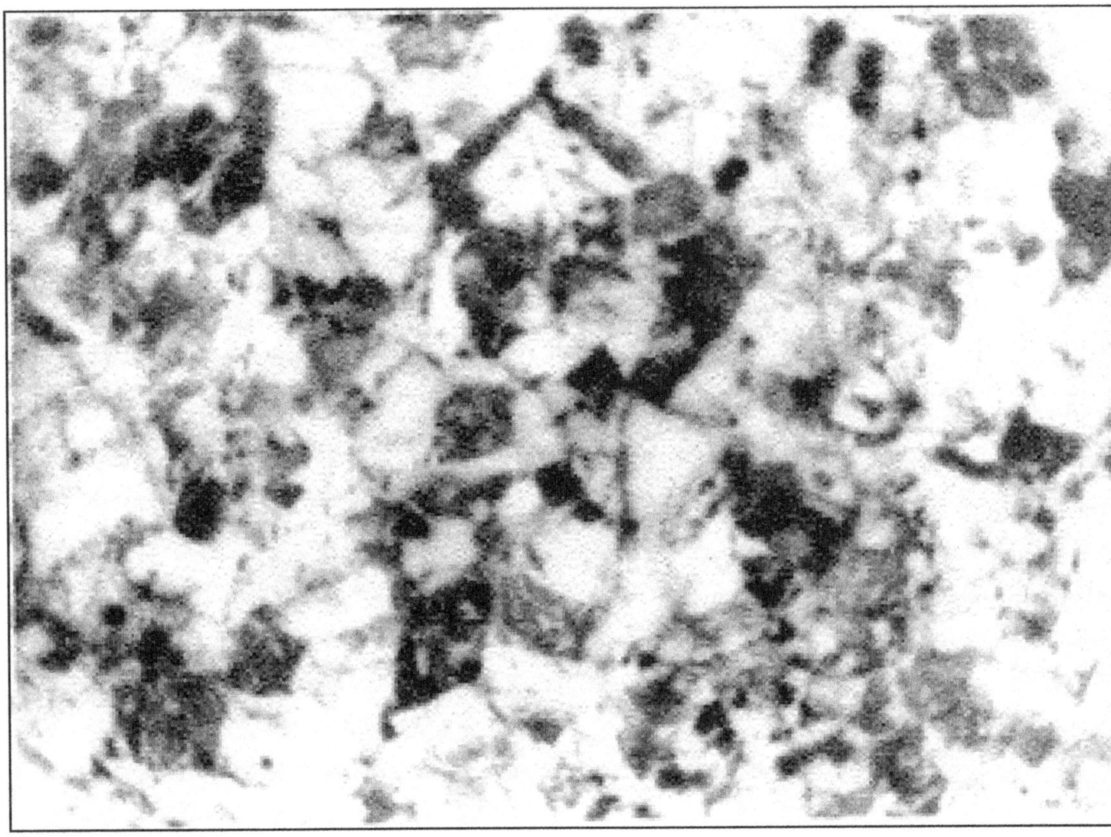

The pictures presented in this section are of two types: the large rogfogo/rokfoto sheets which were all in one packet sent by Richard Shaver to Ray Palmer, and zoomed-in, excerpted images which were found embedded in the 33 larger rogfogo images. Shaver would often send both photo-positive and photo-negative exposures, claiming that different images would be revealed by doing so.

Excerpted images may not be on the same page as the larger rogfogo sheet from which they were excerpted. The reader should feel free to look for them at will, and possibly find others that were not presented here. A helpful hint: the embedded images can be found by rotating the page in any direction.

Shaver's personal cosmology included reptilian humanoids, merpeople/aquatic humanoids, mighty Amazon warriors, spacemen, aliens of various sorts, subterranean humanoids, robots, and animal-human hybrids. All of these types of strangely archetypal forms can be seen on the following pages, perhaps through the application of just a modicum of imagination.

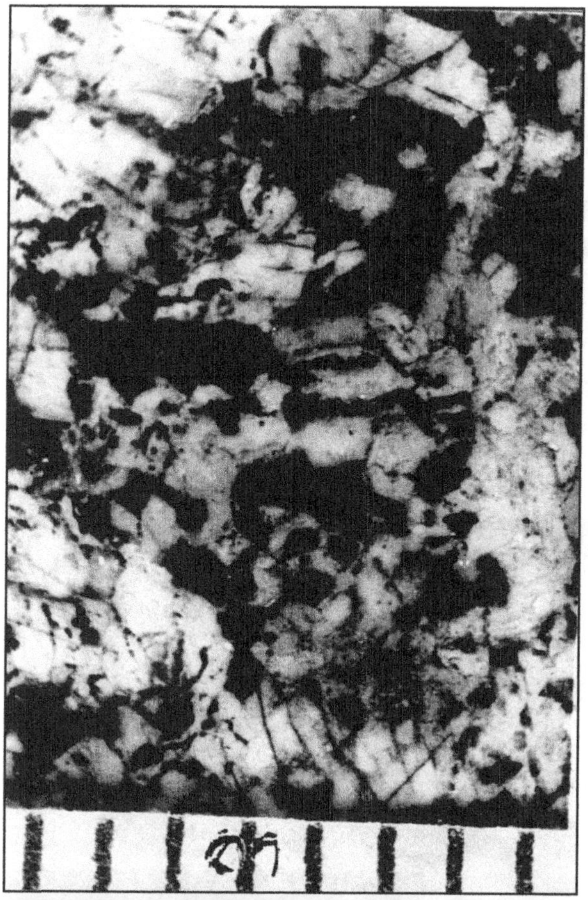

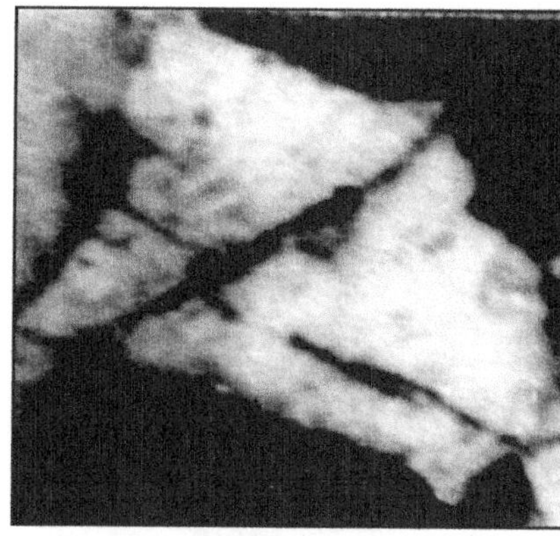

Above: Reptilian Head
in hat or hood.
Two images below: Cluster of
buildings, or cluttered desk?

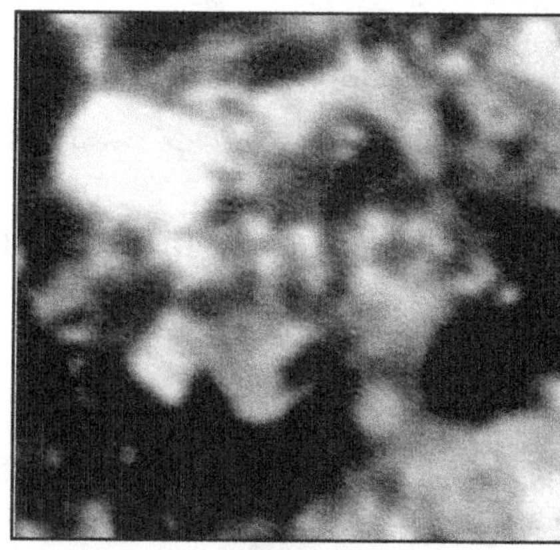

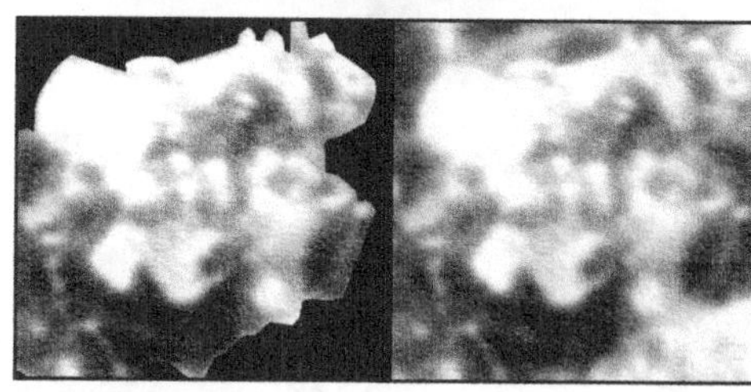

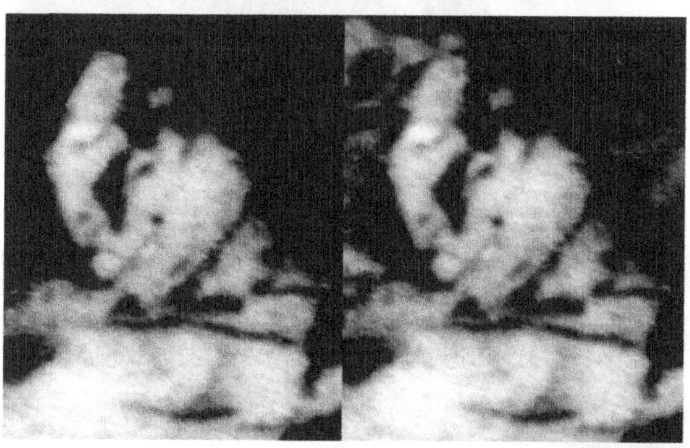

Two Above: The rock
containing the images
on this page
Directly above: A distorted,
smiling head and neck,
rotated downward.
Right: A smiling dinosaurian
head..

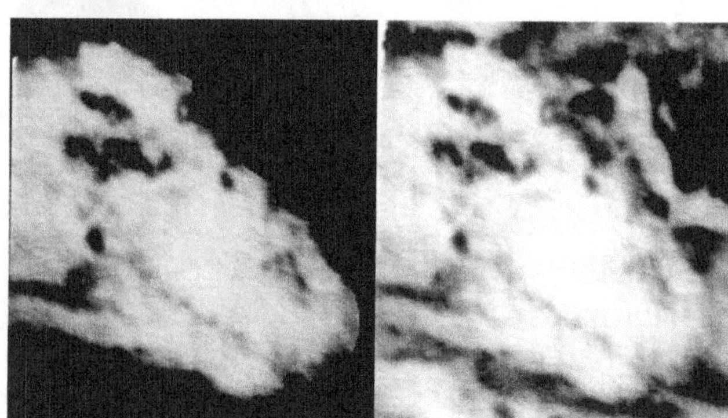

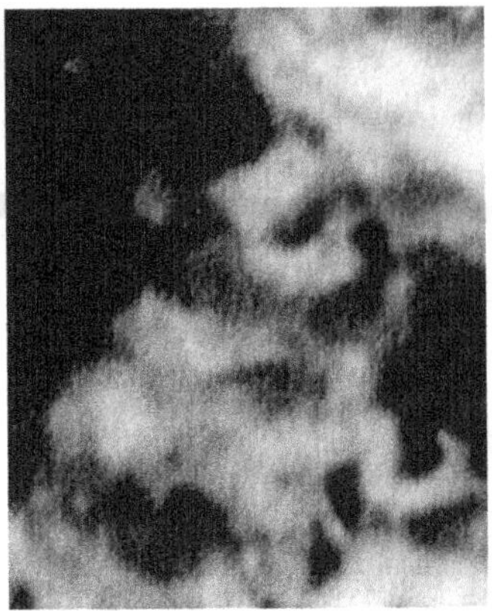

Above: A beastlike being with a pirate-like hook.

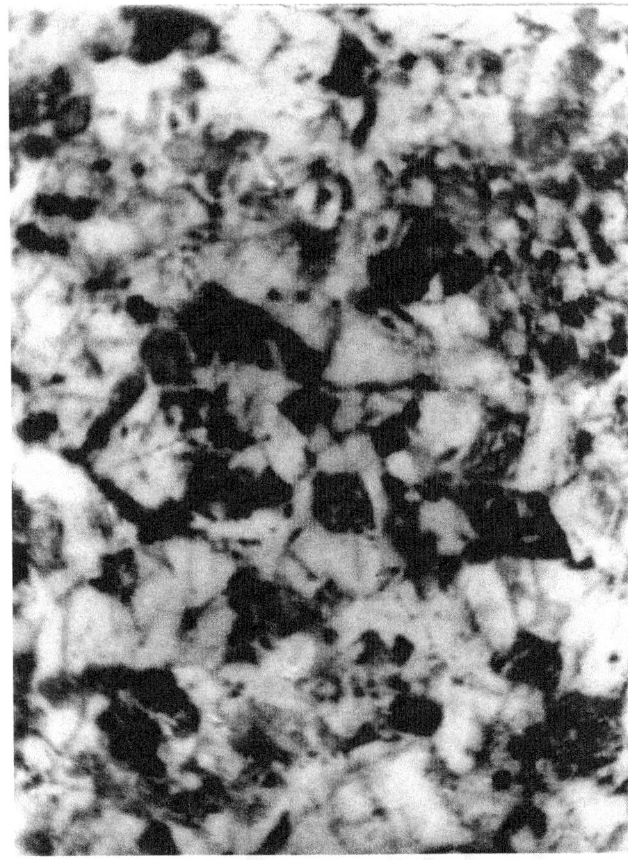

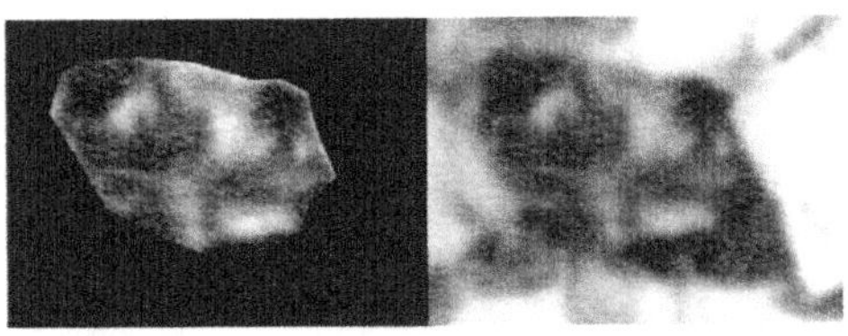

Above: A peeping, large eyed being

Right: A craggy, cubistic face.

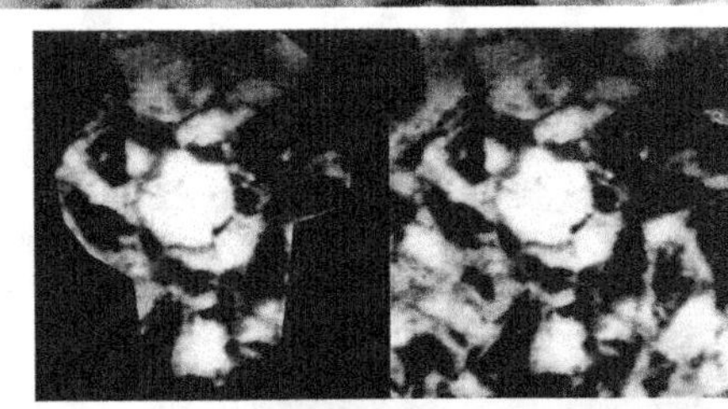

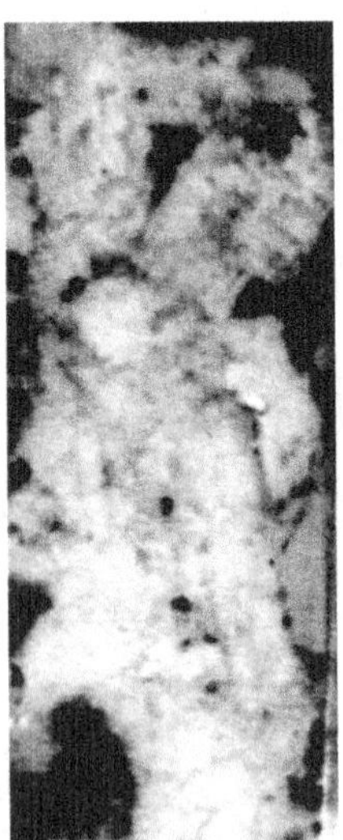

Above: A cartoonish figure with apparatus attached.

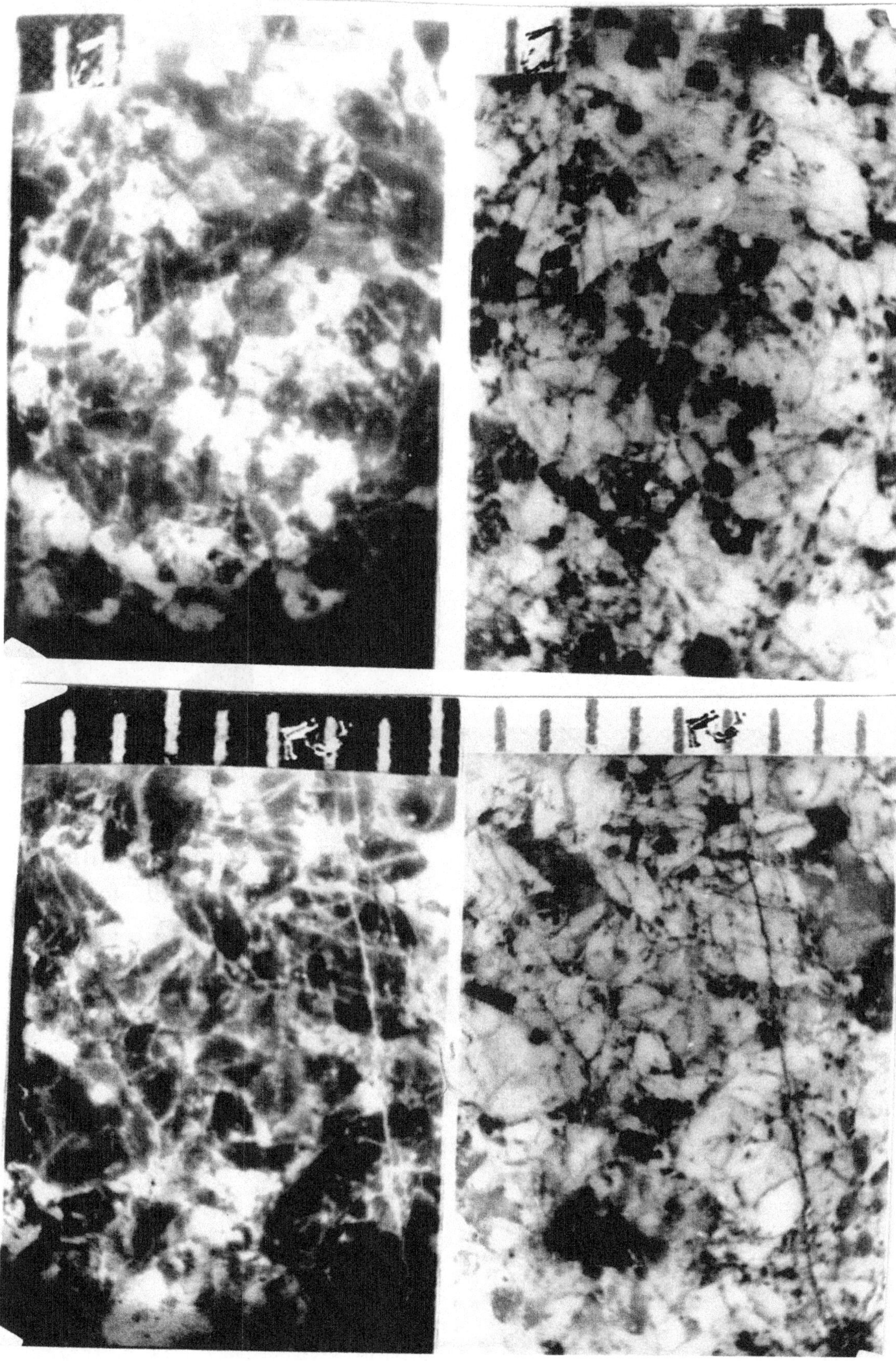

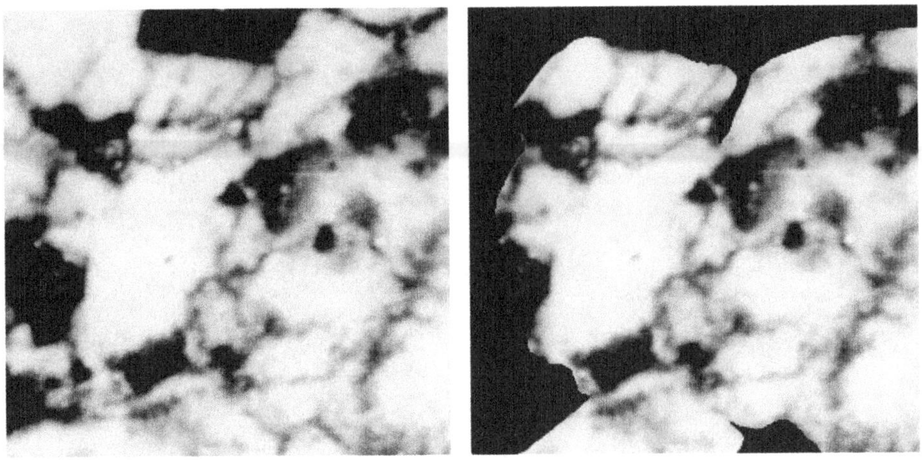

The Two Pictures Above: "Angry Twins".

Right: Pre-Flood "Beauty Queen".

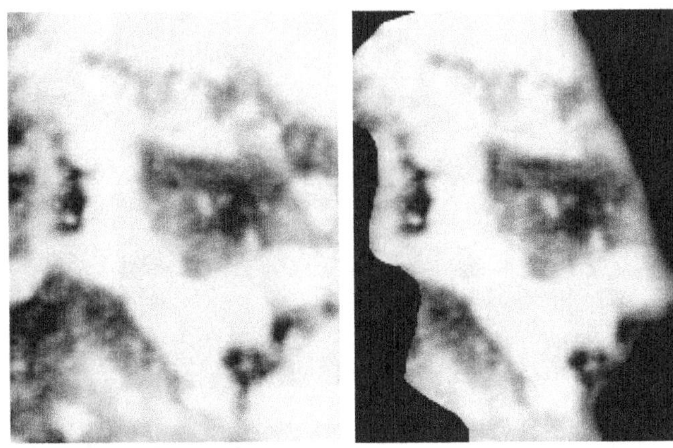

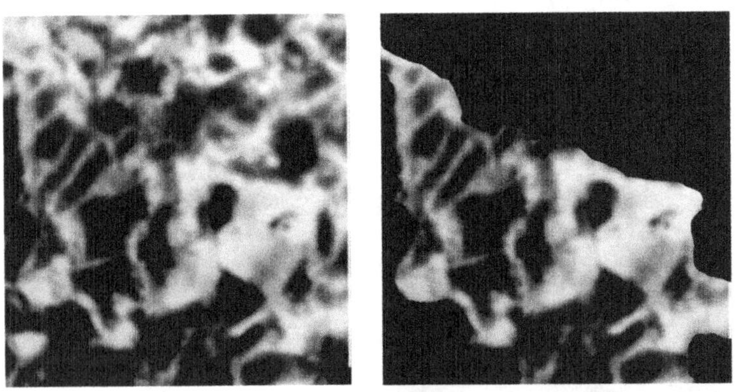

Above: Reclining "Wizard" head.

Right: "Whisperers".

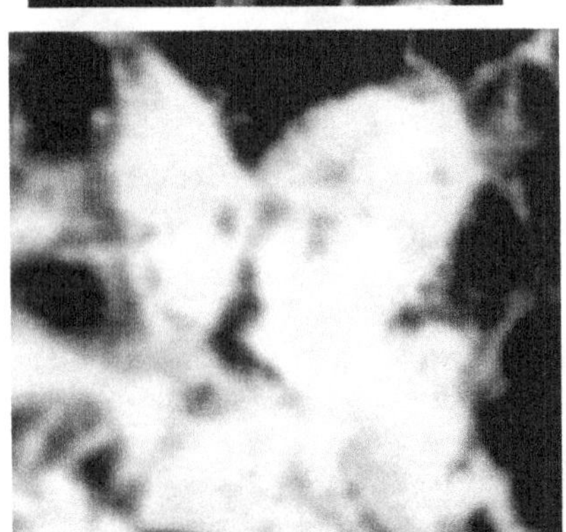

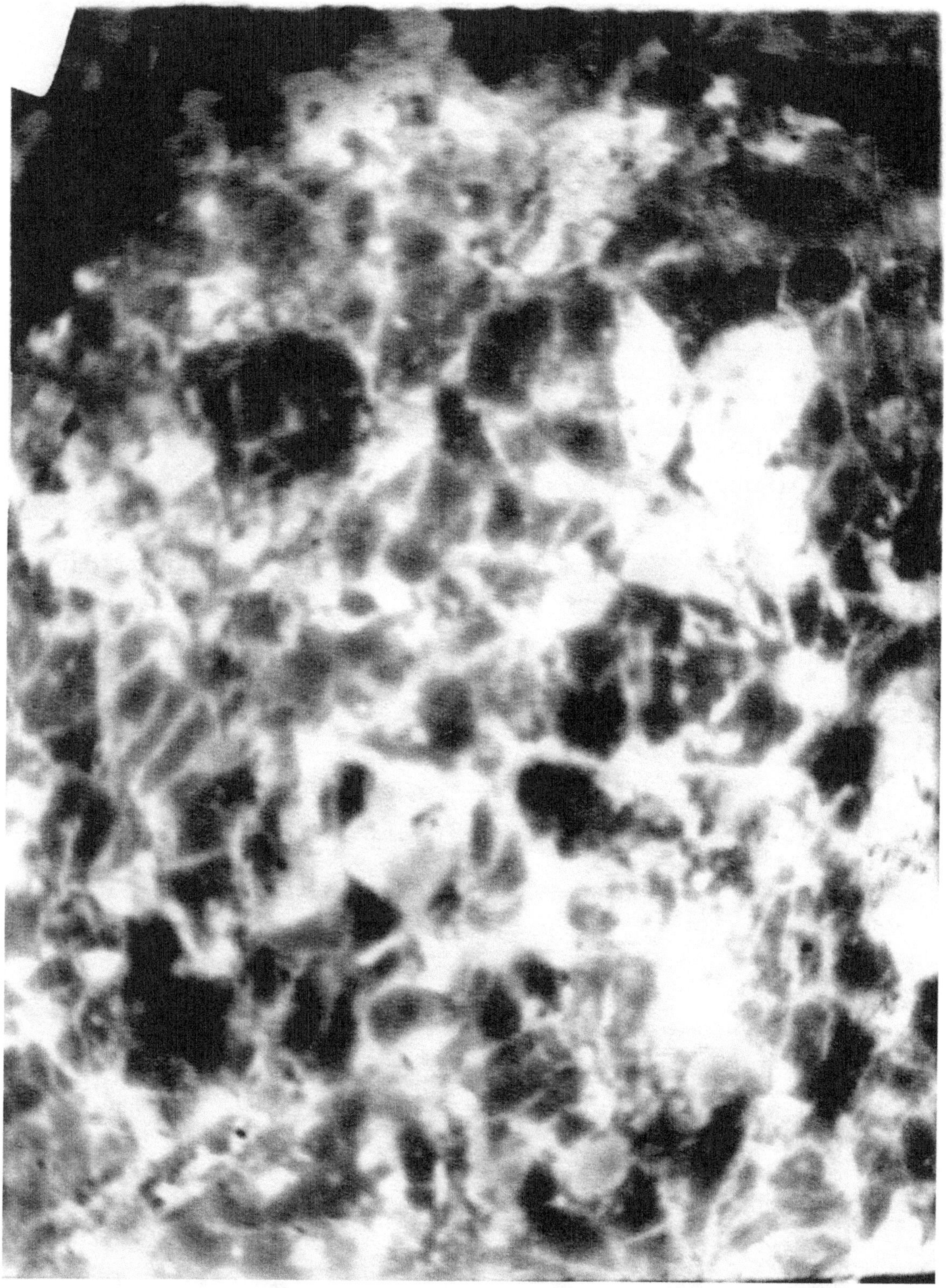

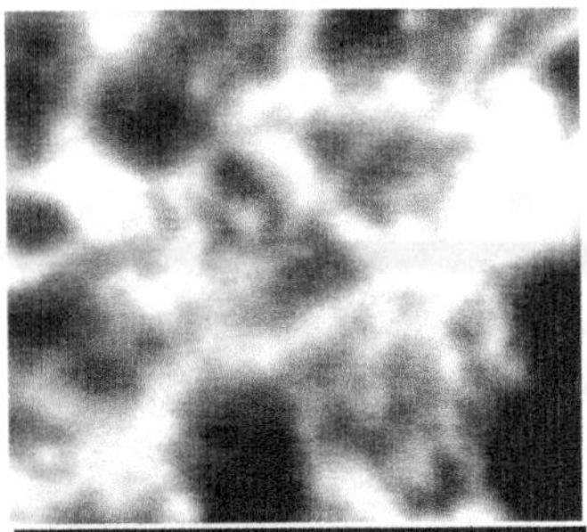

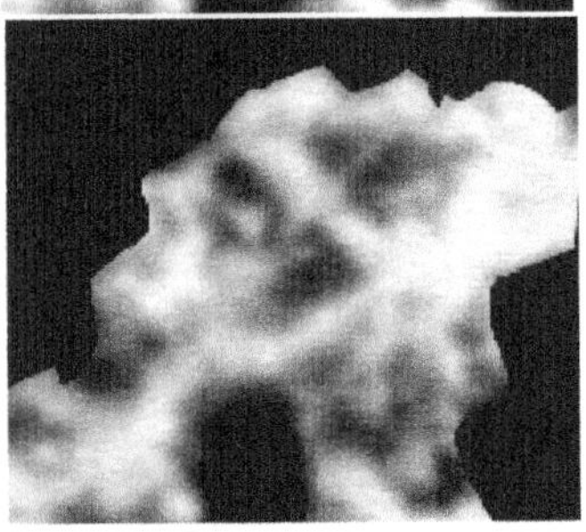

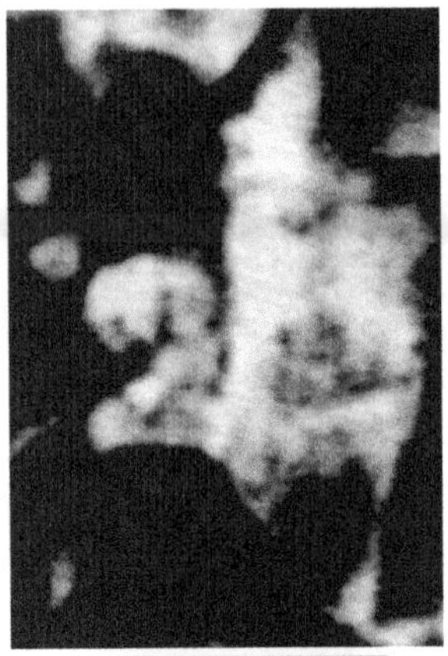

Left:
Cloudy face.
Right:
Small being
with mask,
in stone
chair.

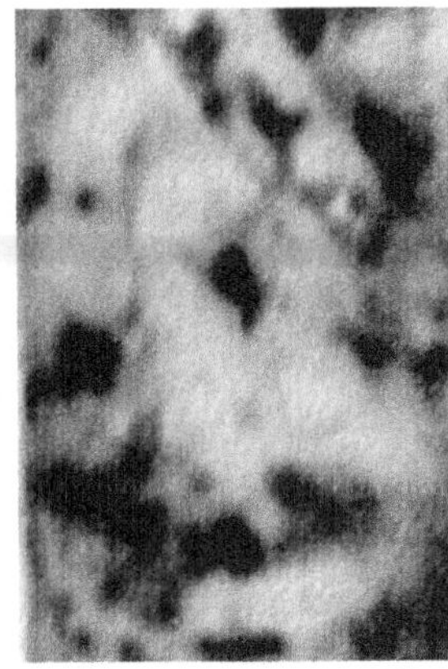

Above: Reclining
"Inca" or Atlantean
King

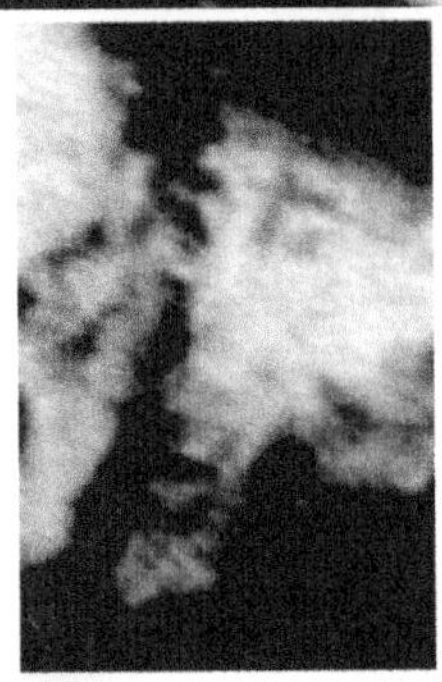

Left: Narrow
face.

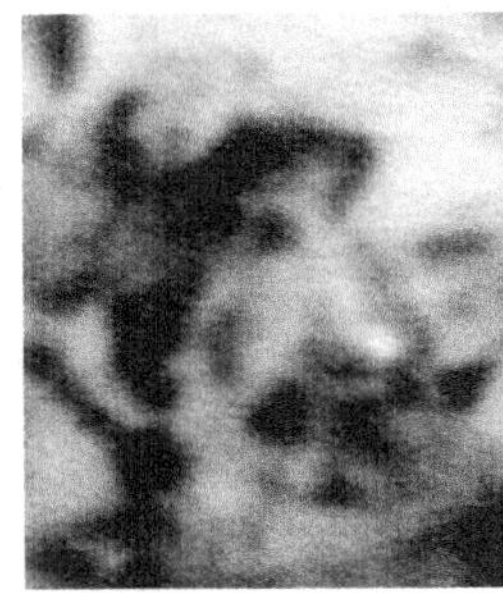

Left:
Partial skull.

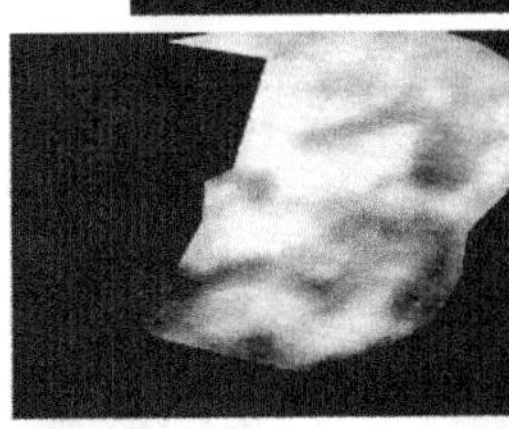

Above: Moai or
Easter Island
head or distorted
human form?

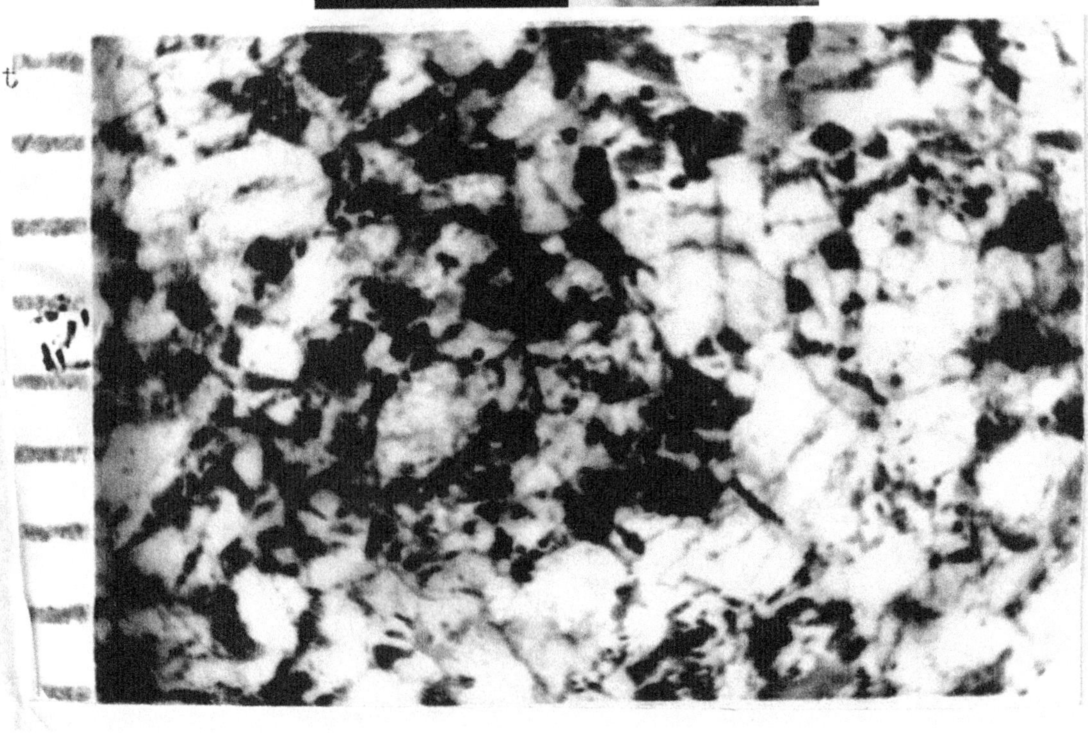

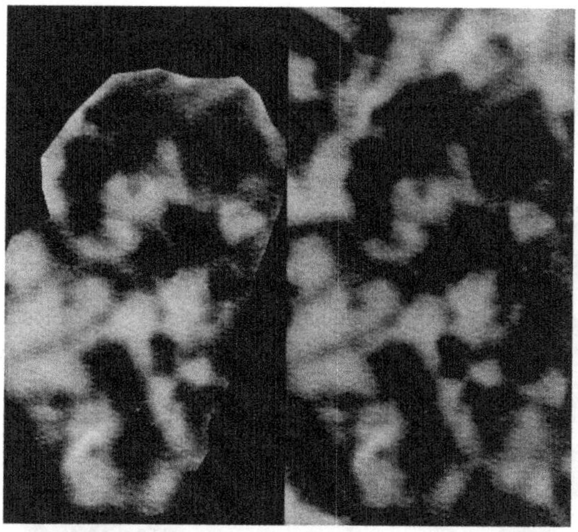

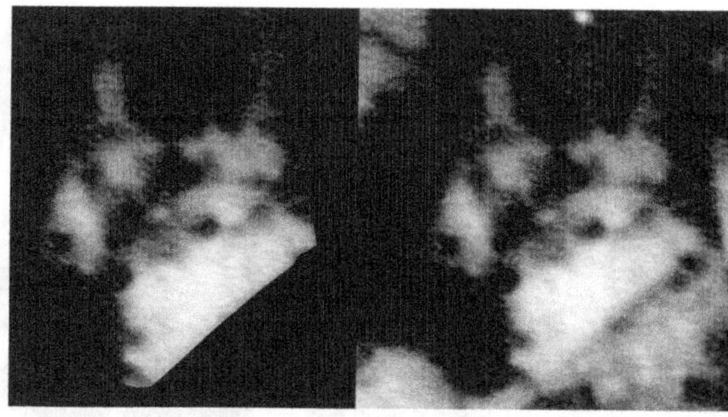

Left: Distorted rocky head and face.
Above: Horned creature or devil head

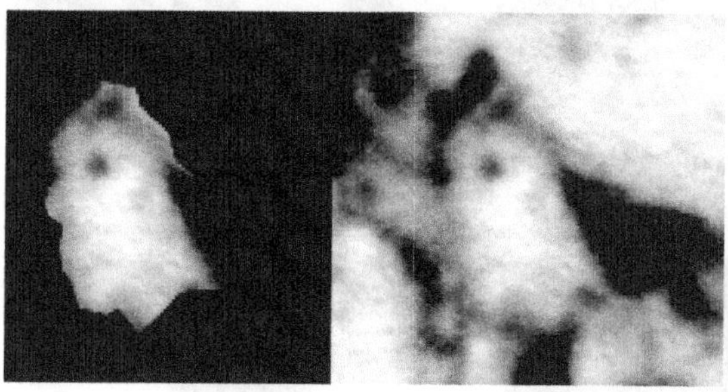

Above: Long-faced profile.

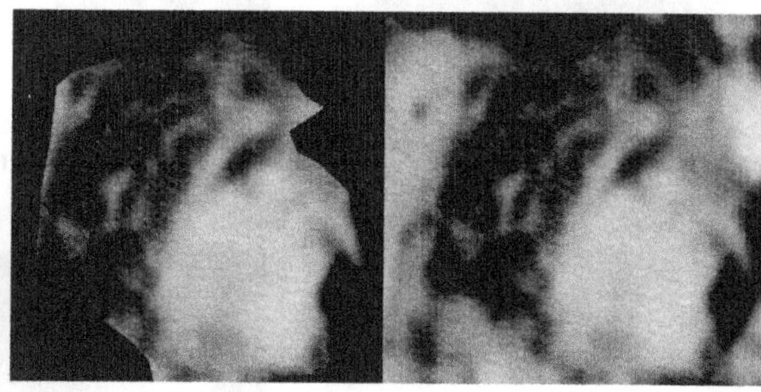

Above: "Long-nosed" dero (a theme from Shaver's writing).

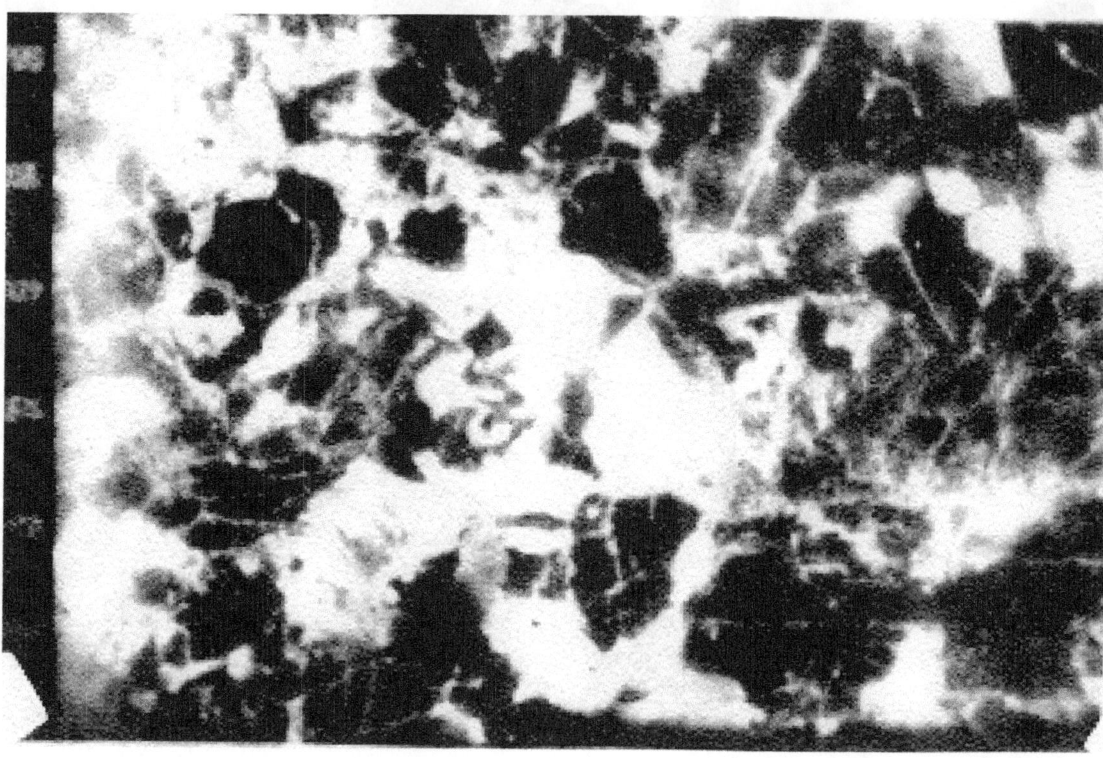

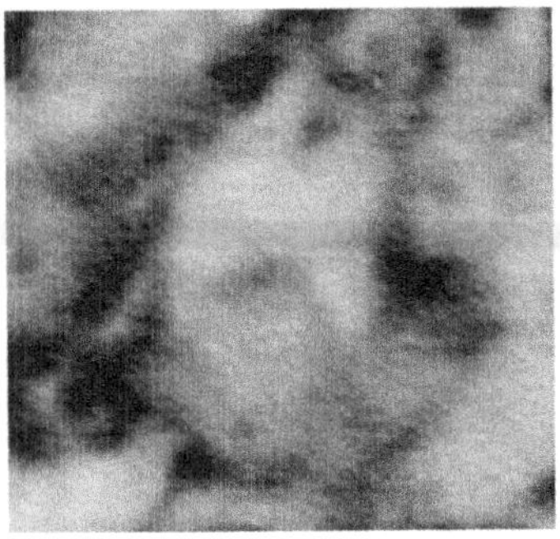

Above and Below: Strange faces.

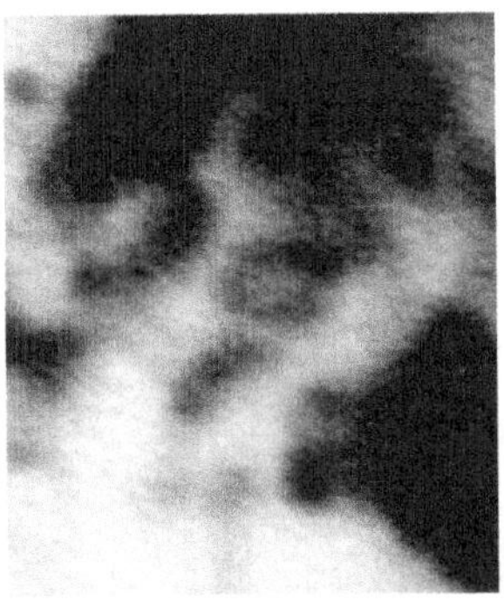

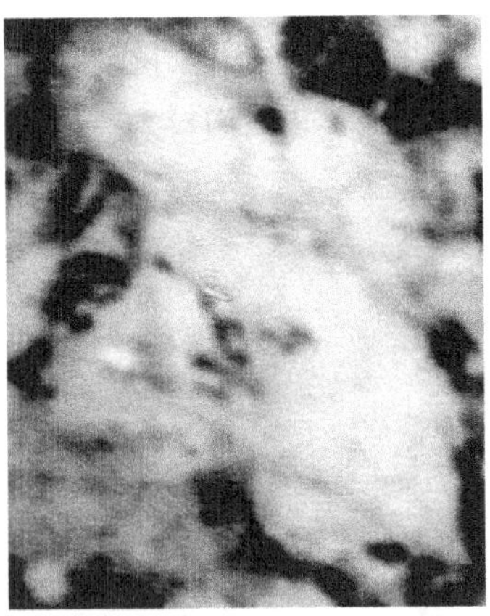

Below: Fat man's head in brimmed hat.

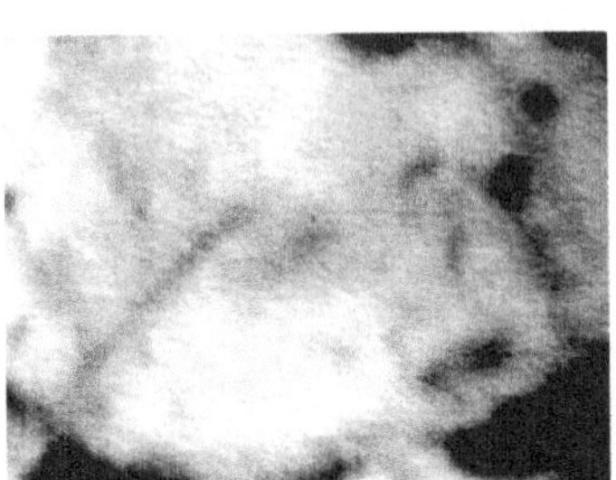

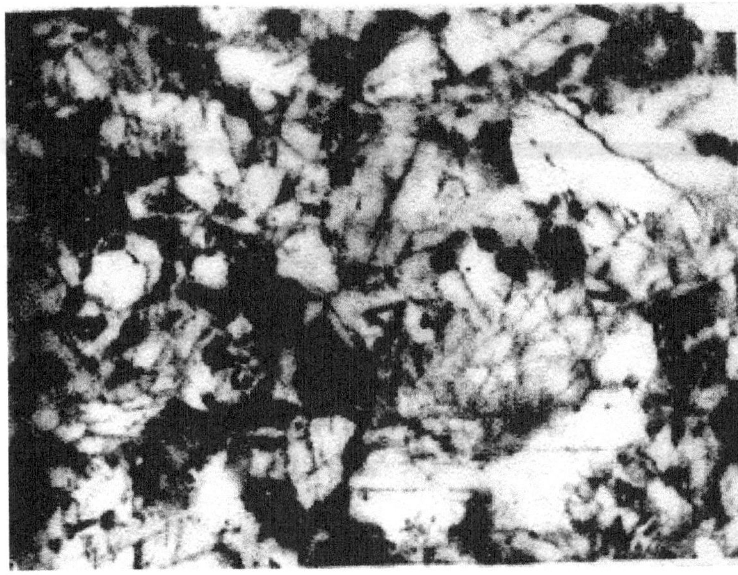

Below: Woman from the back.

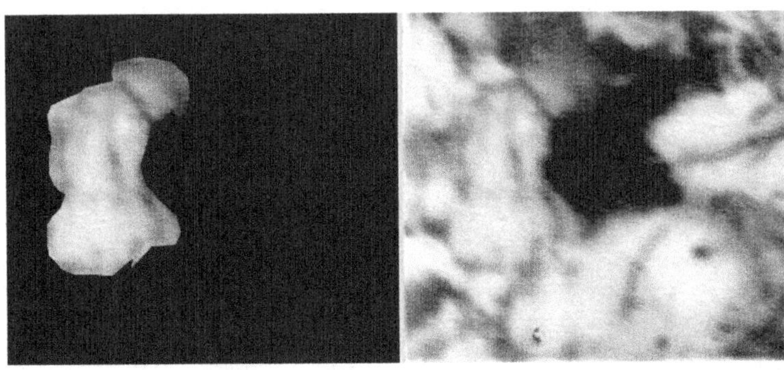

Below: One of Shaver's "ape-bats" or flying monsters.

Left: Cluster of strange heads.

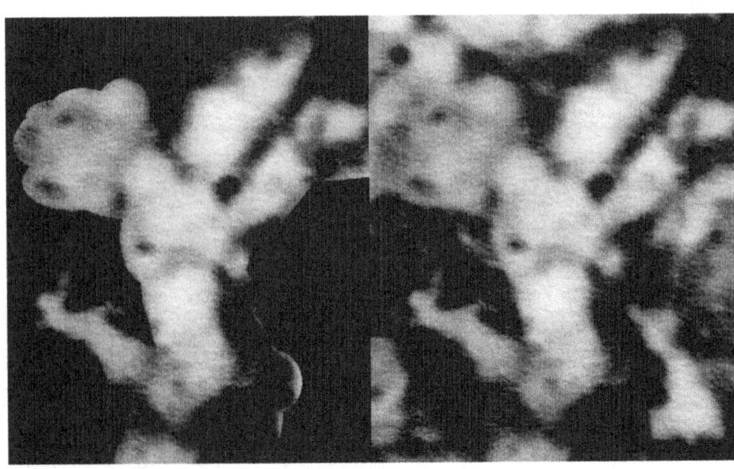

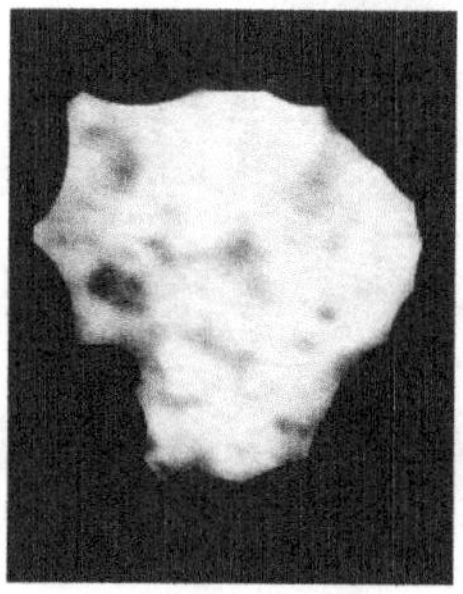

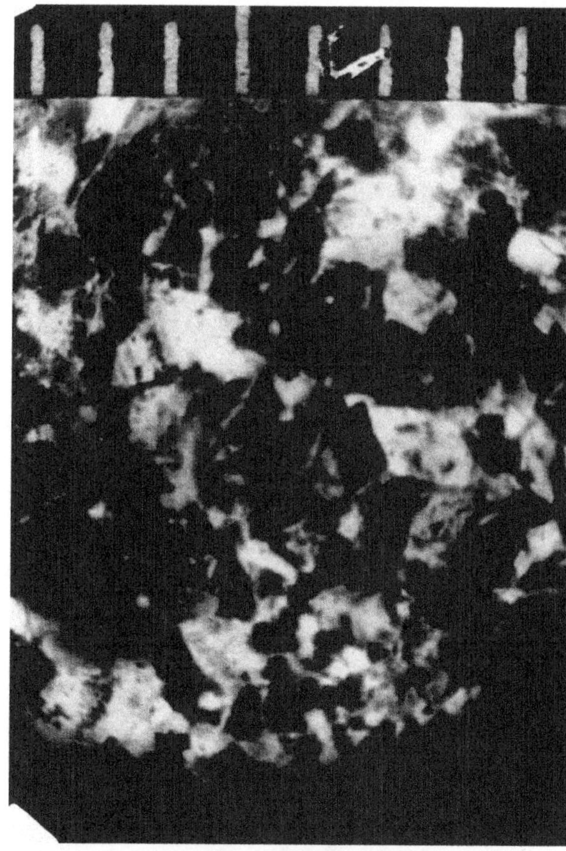

Two Pictures Above: two weird faces, one cat-like, the other with horns (in foreground).

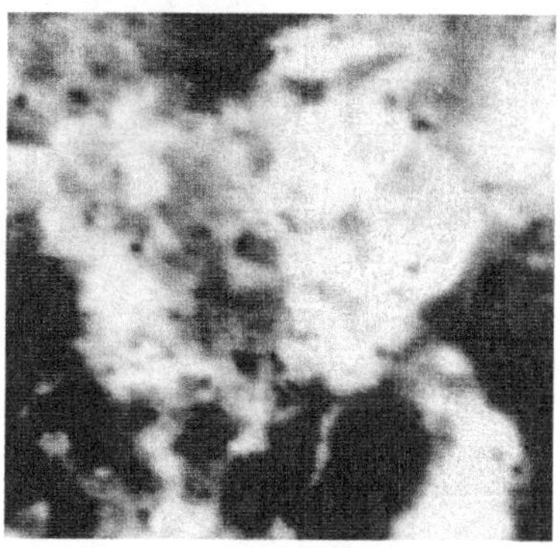

Above: the fragmented face of an old woman.

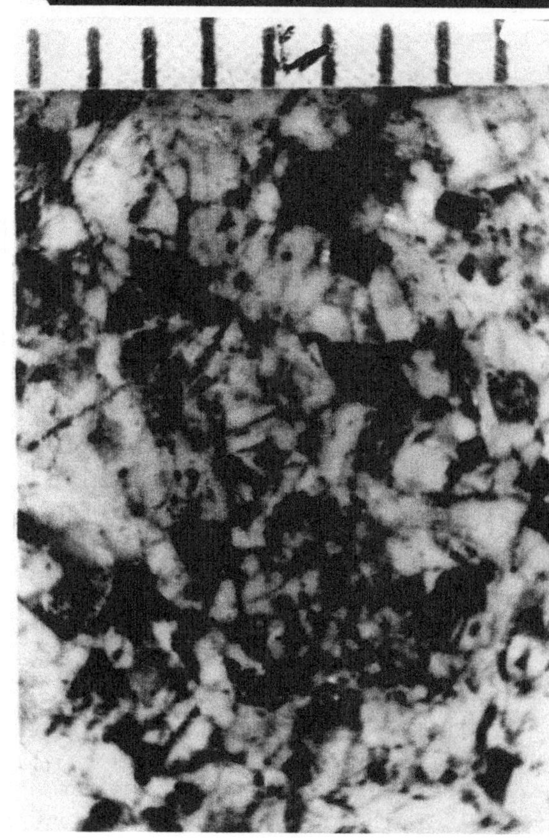

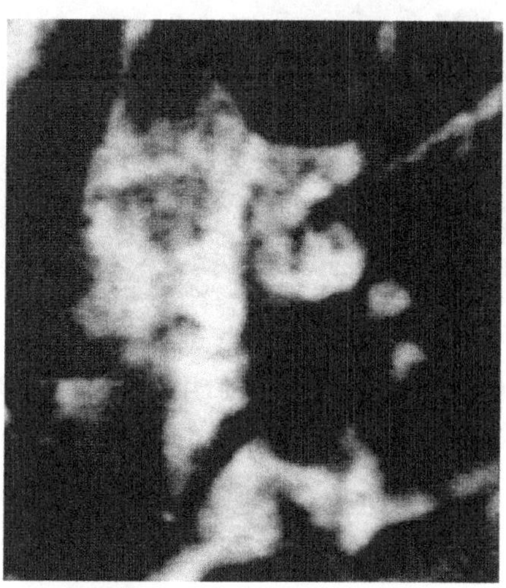

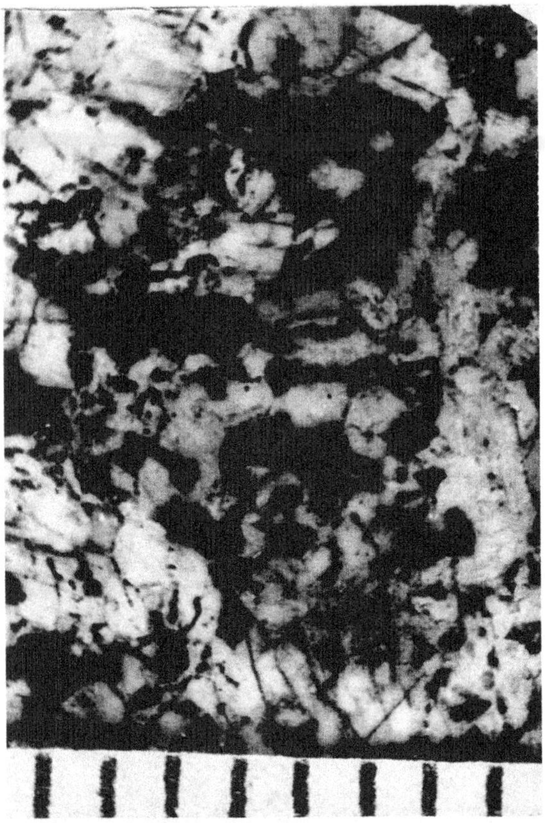

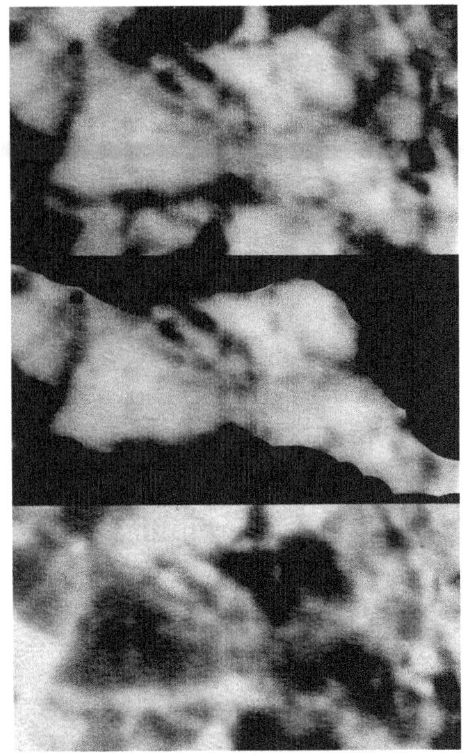

Above: A dismembered female form.

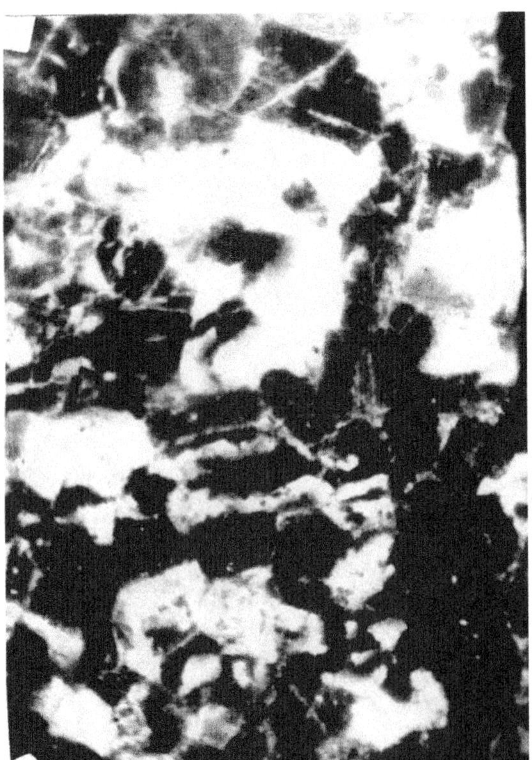

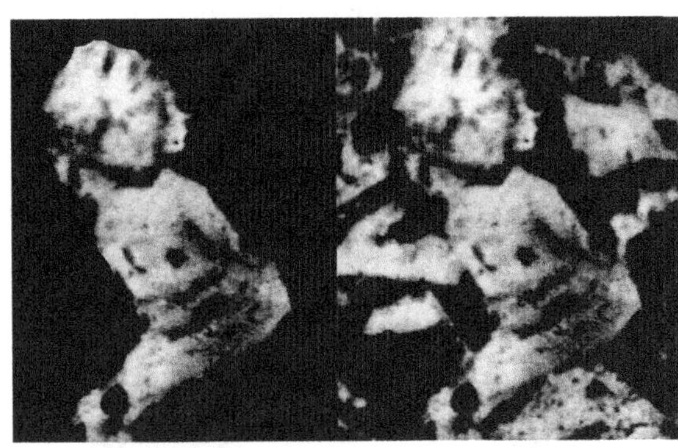

Above: Kneeling woman in kimono -style robe.

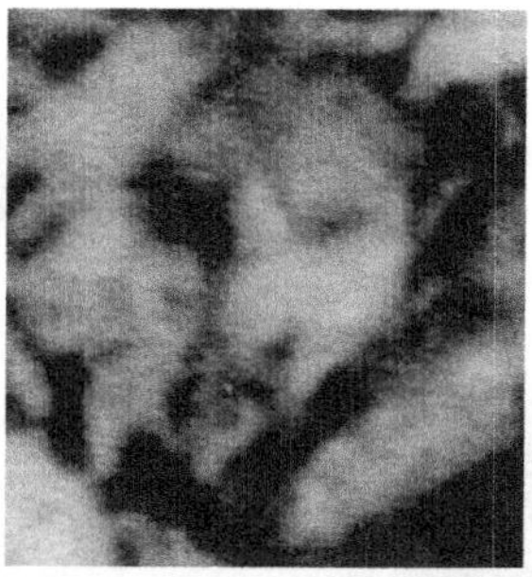

Above: Angular face.
Below: Waving male .

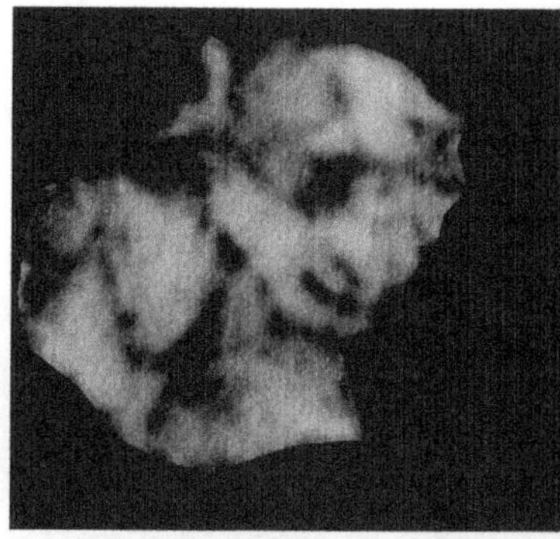

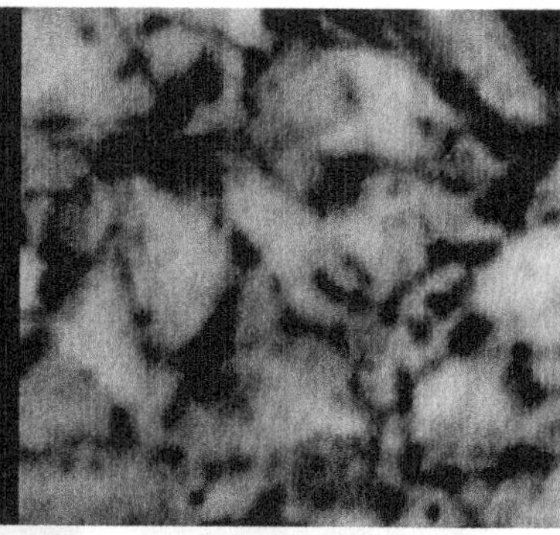

Above: A large-eared, horned being.
Below: Seated nude female, seen from above.

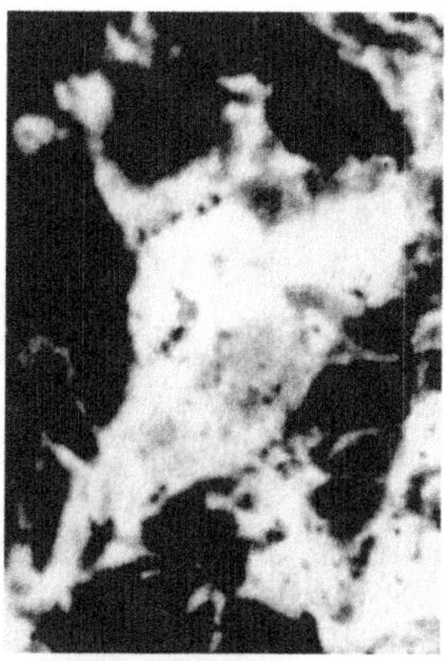

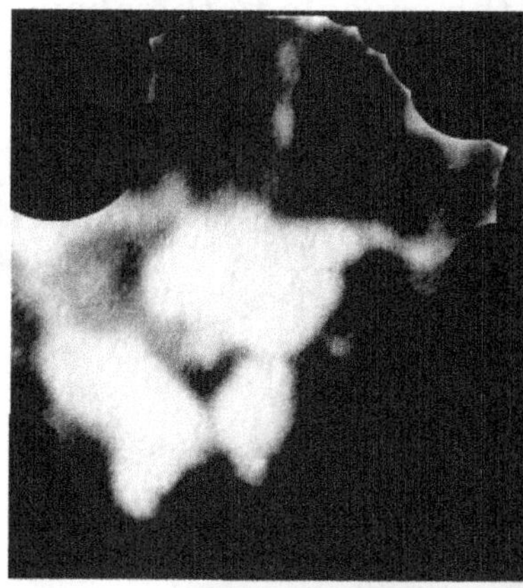

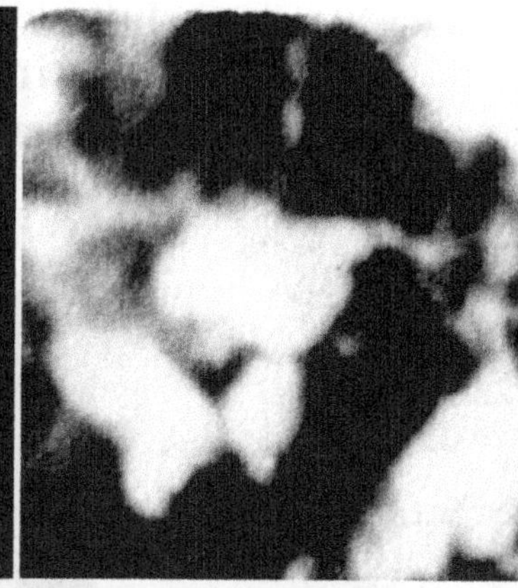

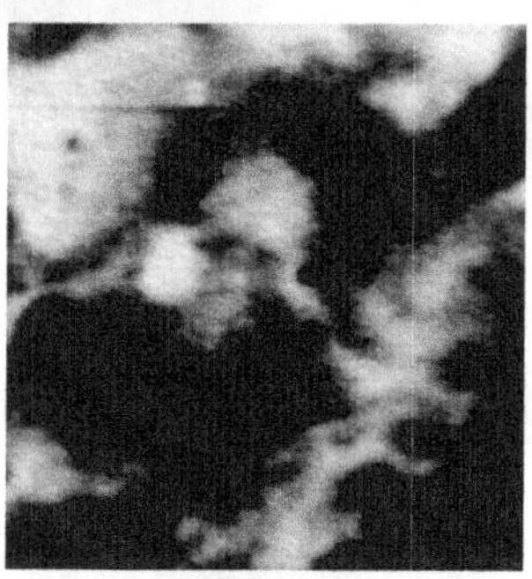

Above/Below: "Peeping dero" profile.

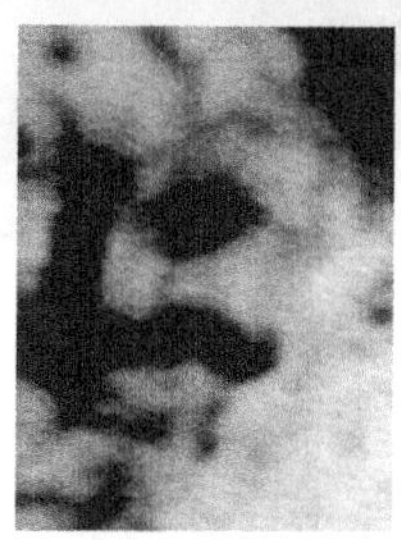

Above: Moustached profile.

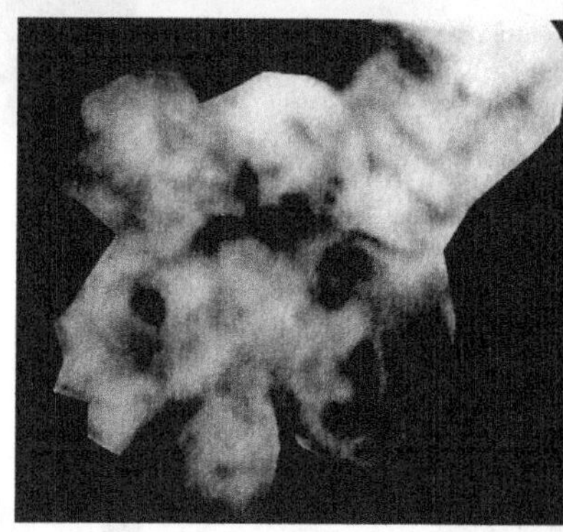

Above/Below: A cluster of faces/heads.

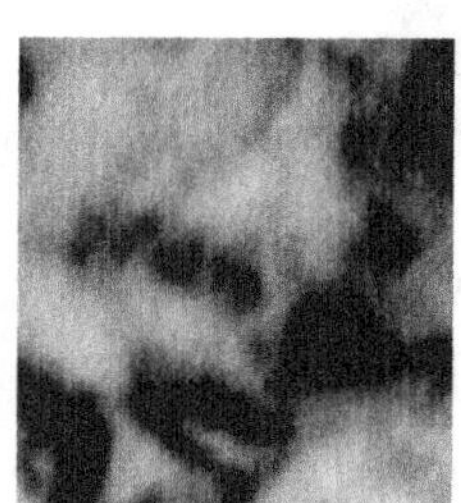

Above: Fish-man face.

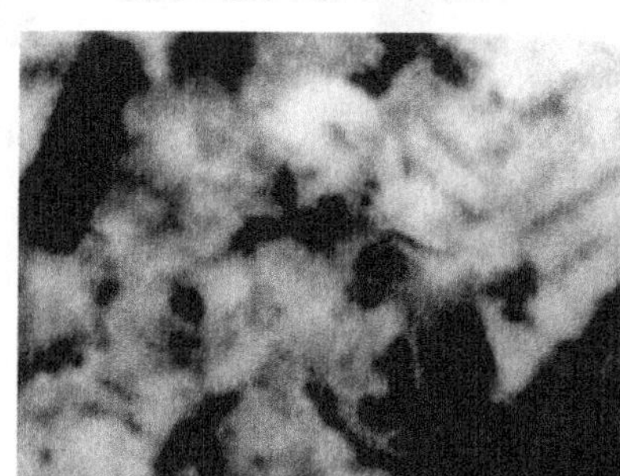

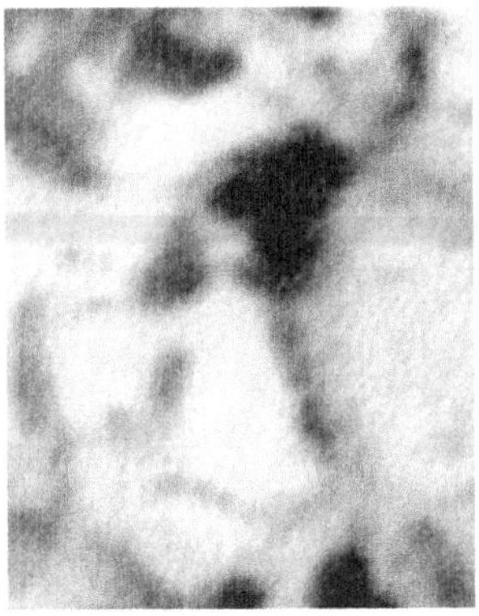

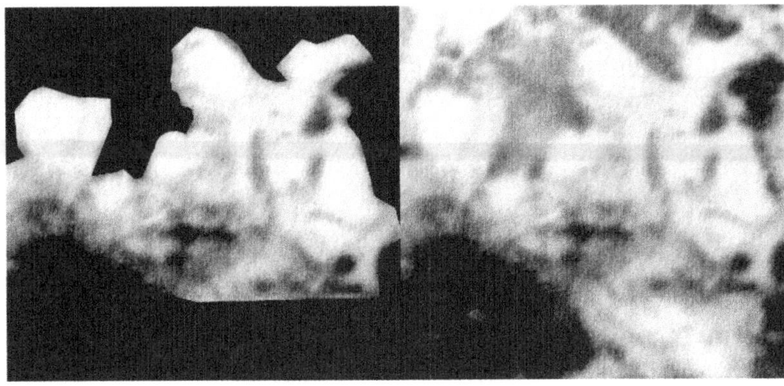

Above Left: Figure in entrance? Possibly the figure is a technician or pilot at the console to the above right..

Below: Gnomish "imp" crouching on rug and looking backward.

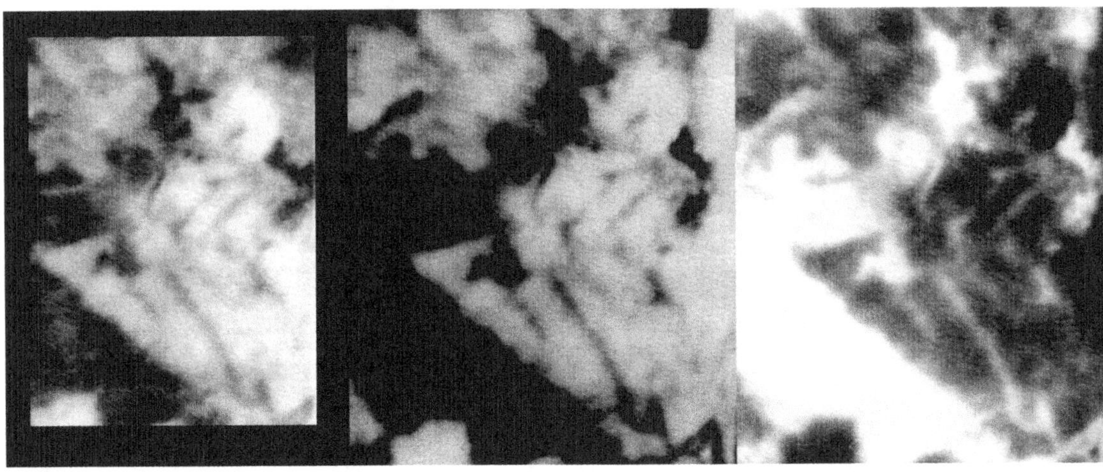

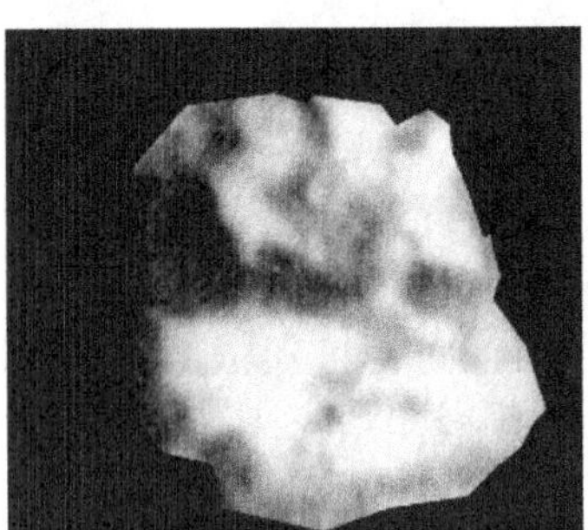

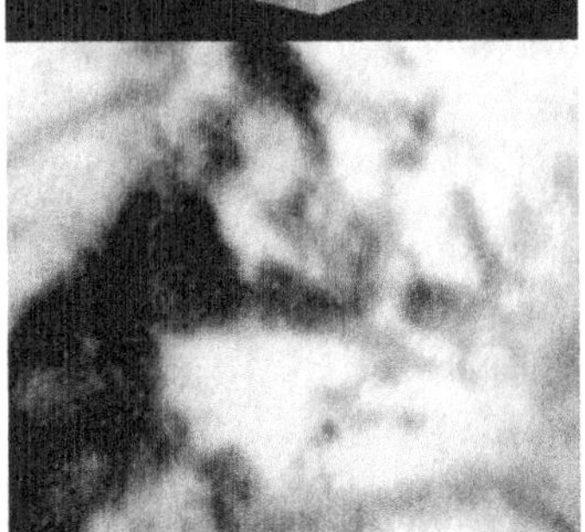

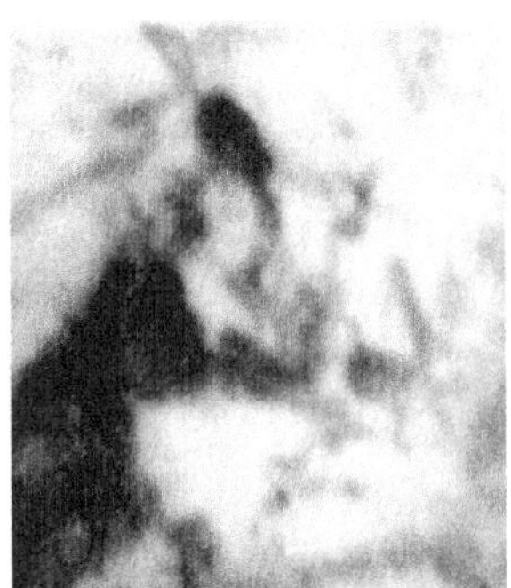

Above: Lady in hat, at desk or vanity? Left: Same picture as above cropped to reveal "stone head".

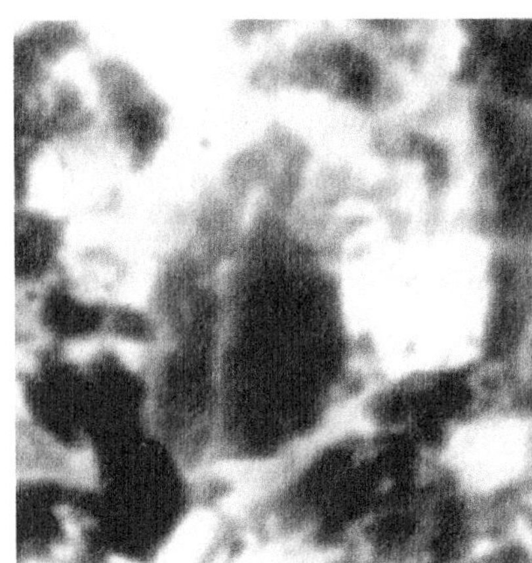

Above: Arched cavern/ tunnel entrance.

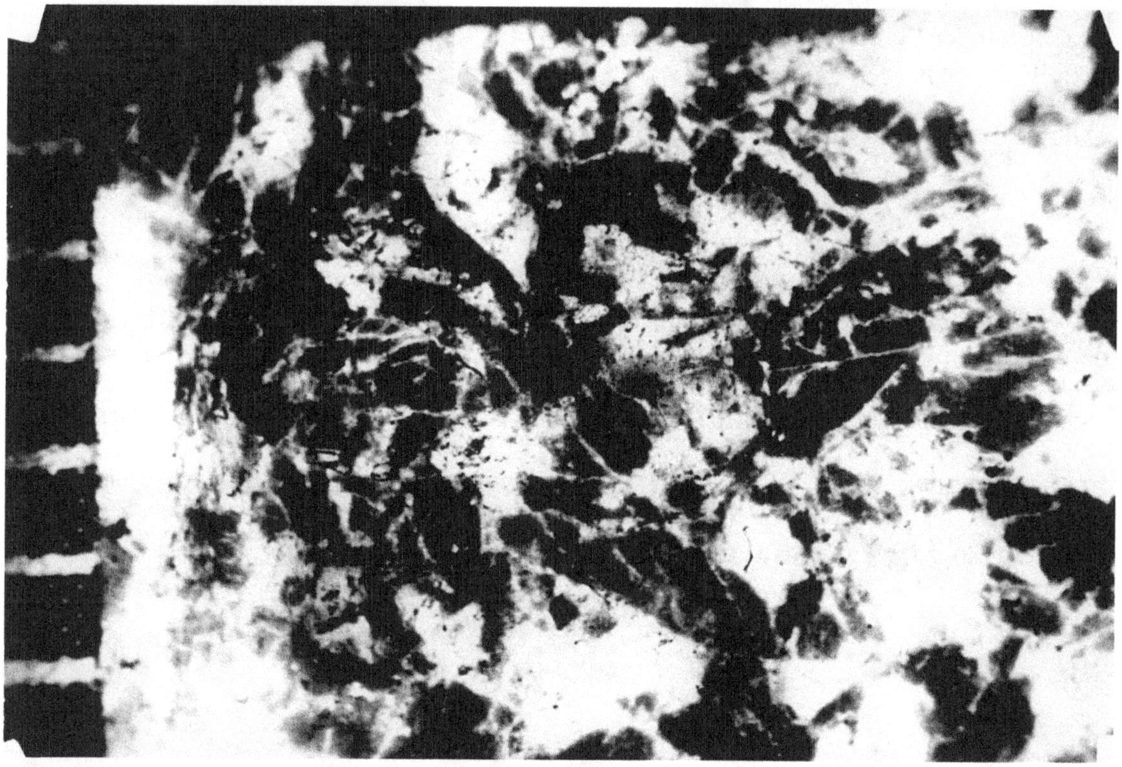

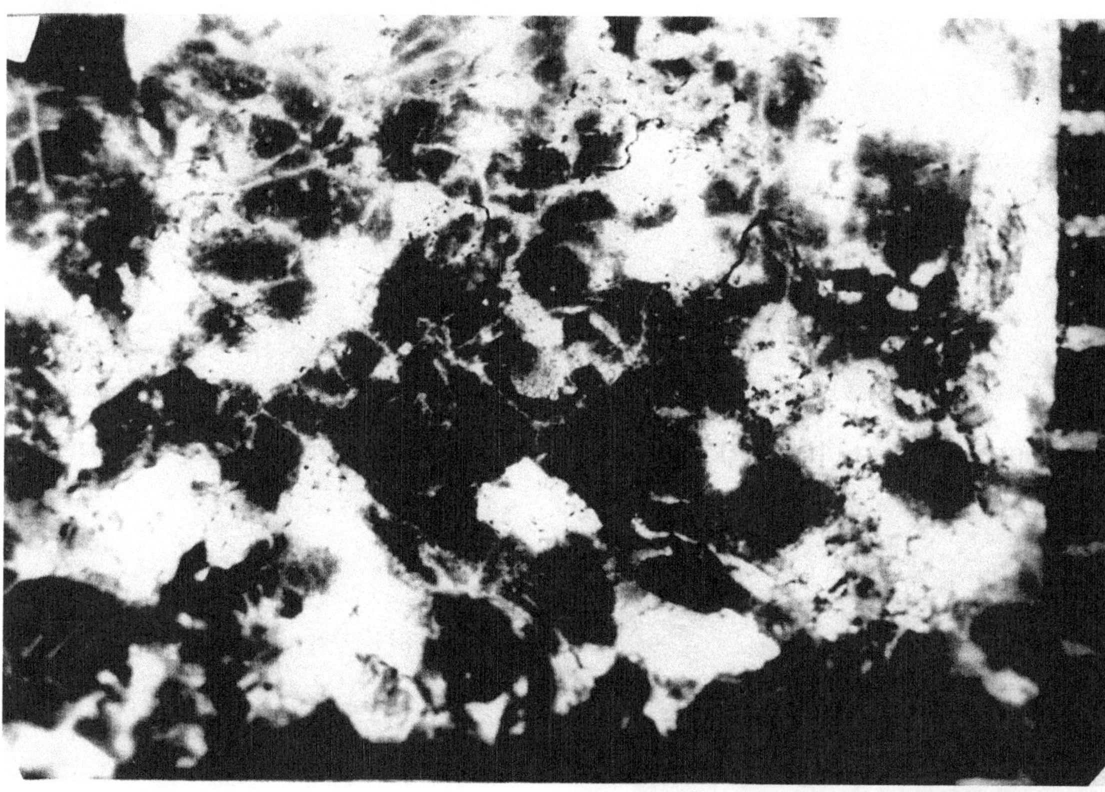

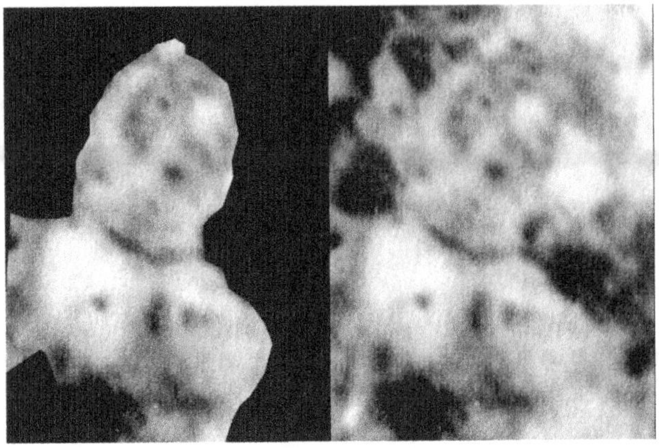

Above: Reptilian woman/humanoid.

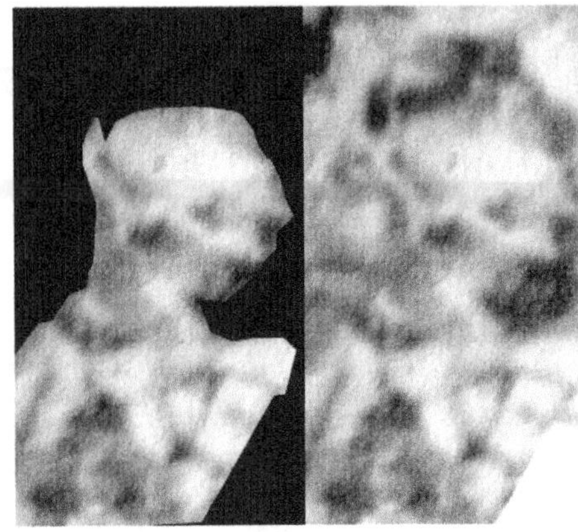

Above: Strange creature

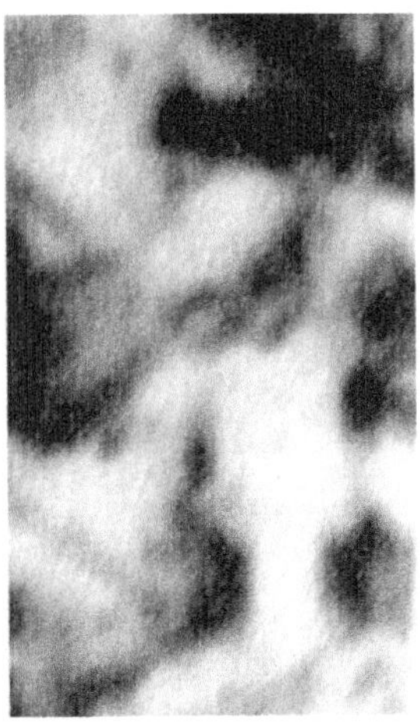

Right: Shaverian "Amazon" fighting beast. Left: A skull on display.

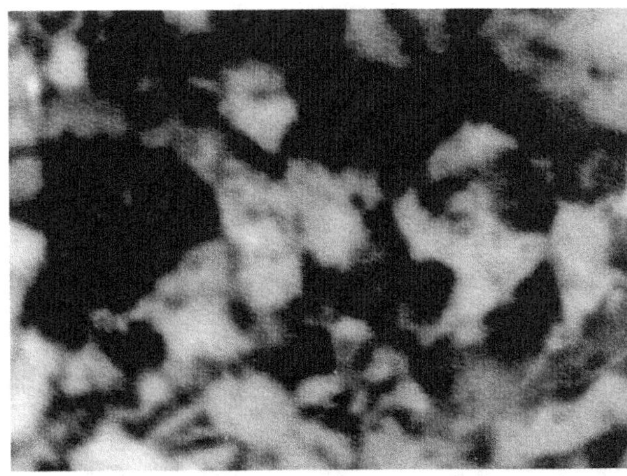

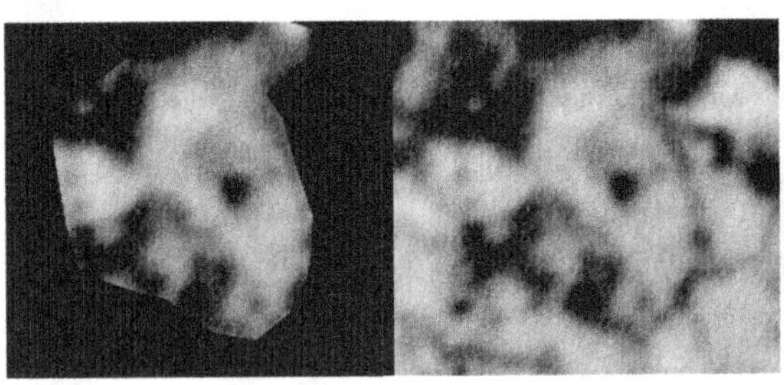

Above: Partial child-like face.

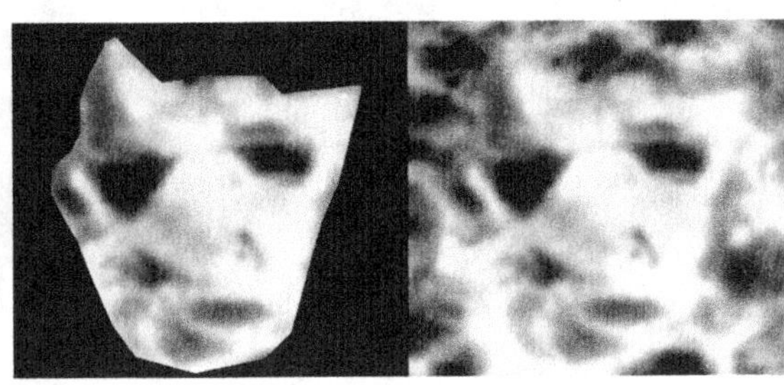

Above: Distorted mask-like face.

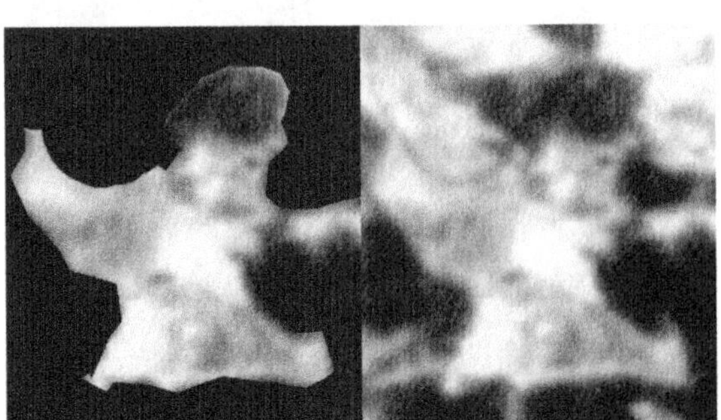

Left: Winged entity.

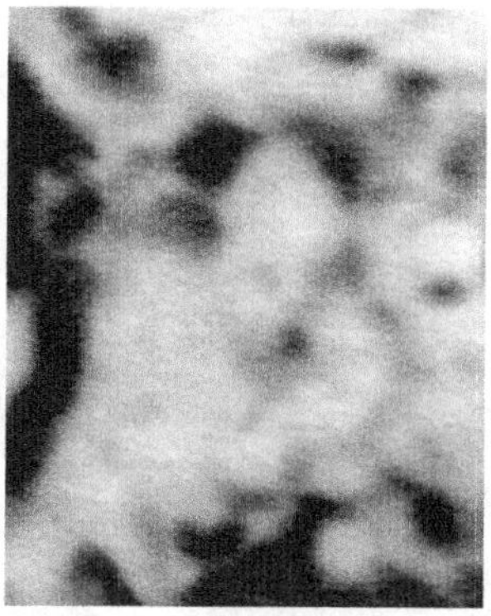

Above: Open-mouthed conehead.

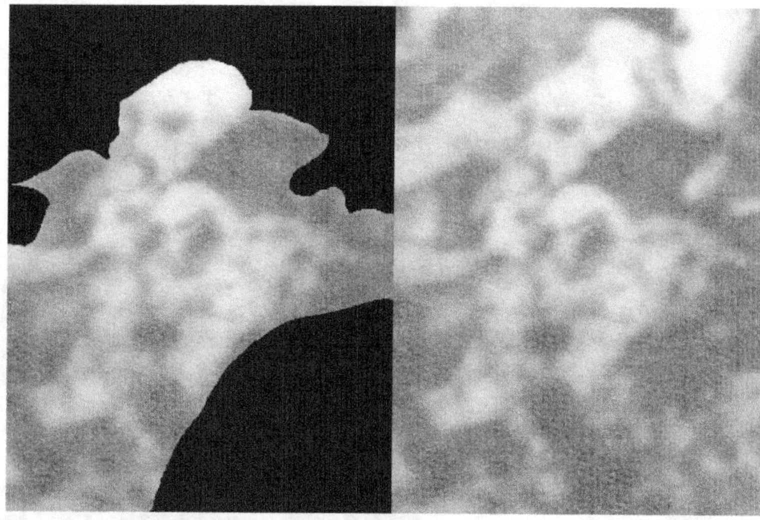

Above: Strange seated figure or being.

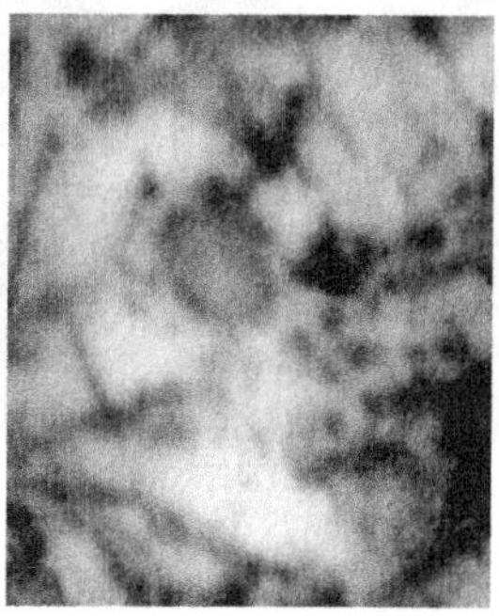

Above: Partial skull "fossil".

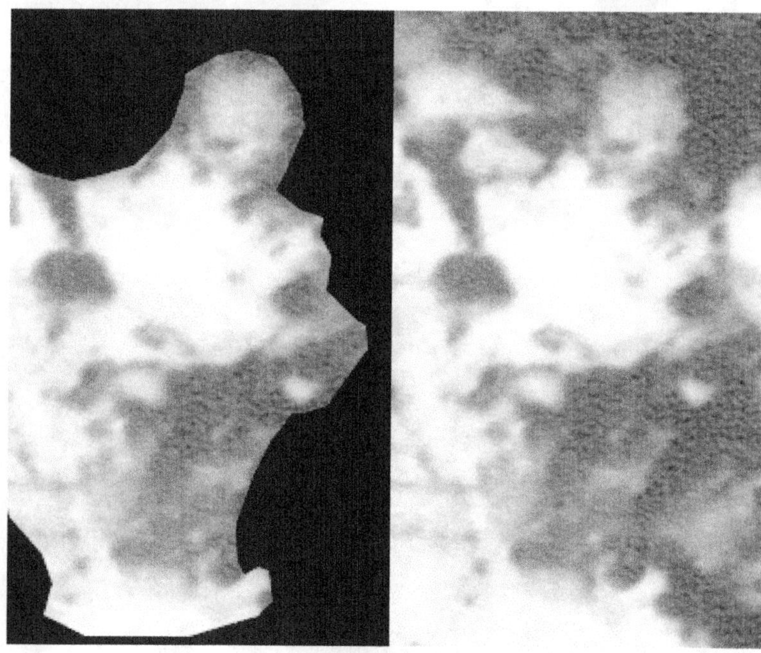

Above: Gape-jawed reptilian monster with dero or imp behind it.

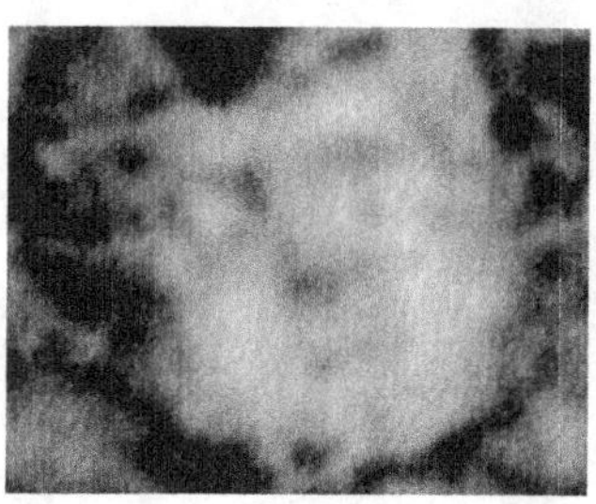

Above: Another face.

Below: Yelling figure.

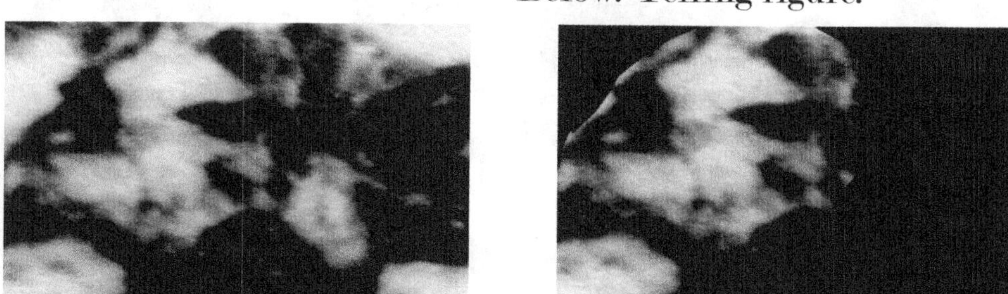

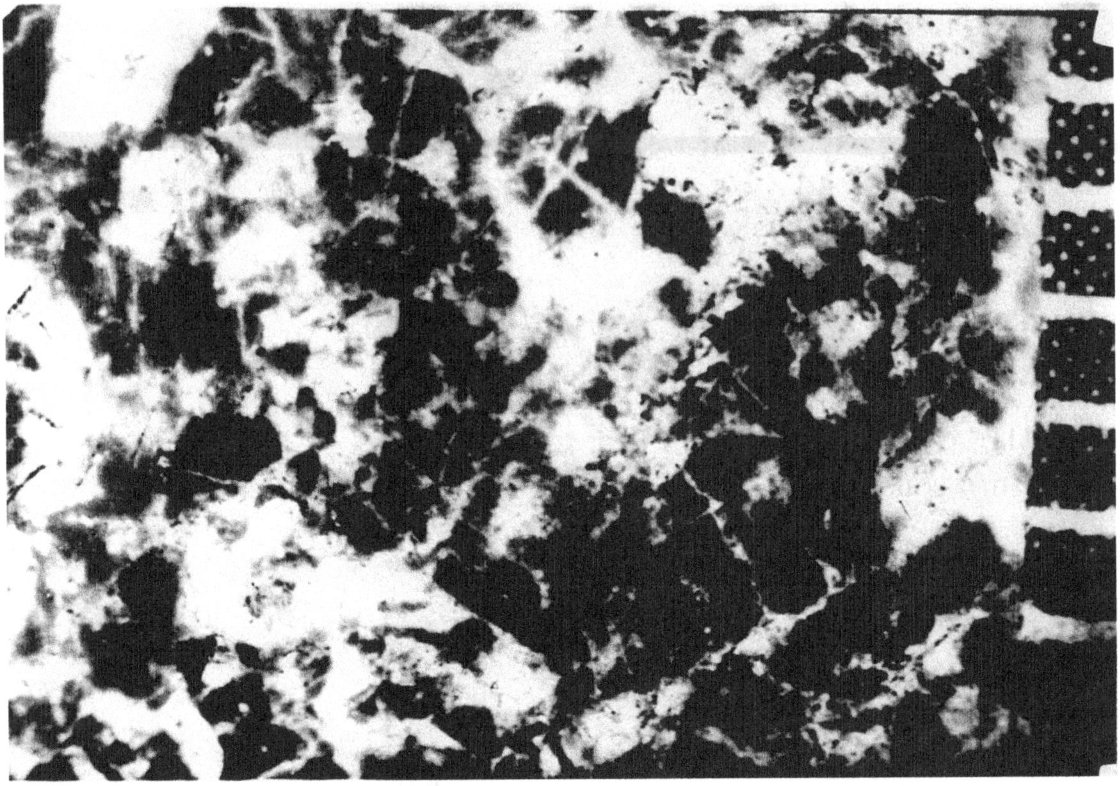

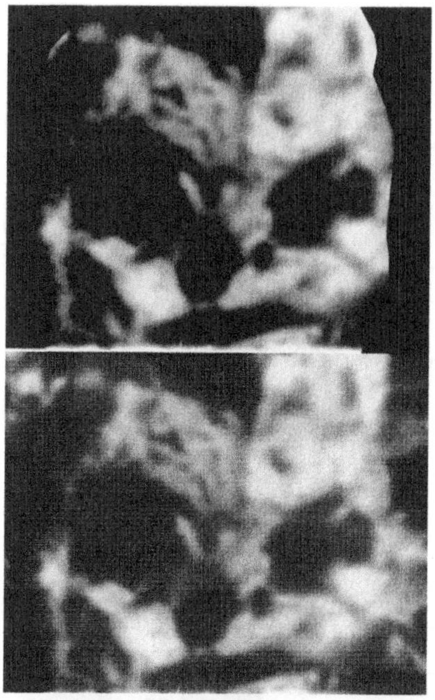

Left: Craggy, rock-like face.
Right: Gape mouthed creatures, devouring something.
Below: Reclining head/face.

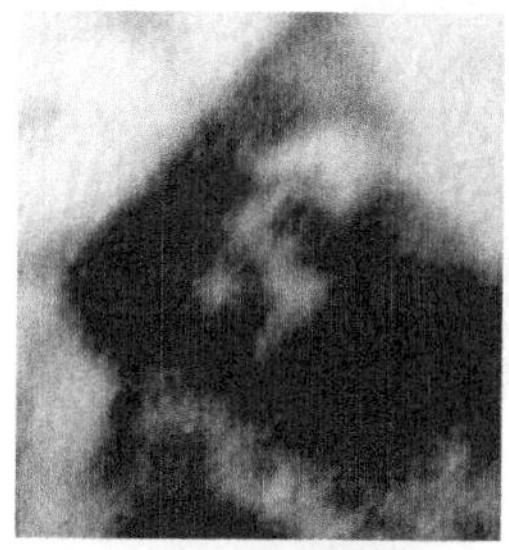

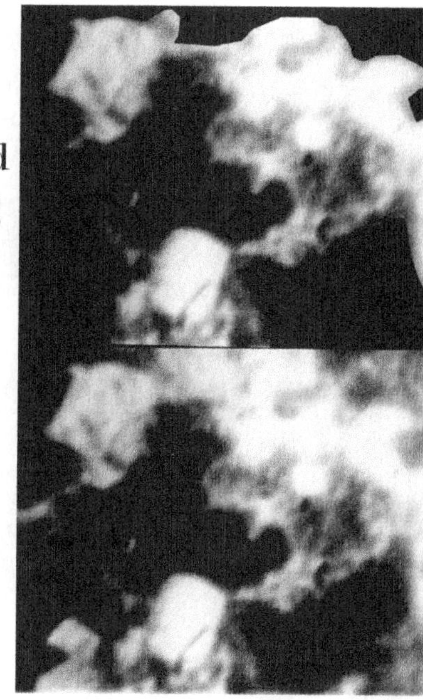

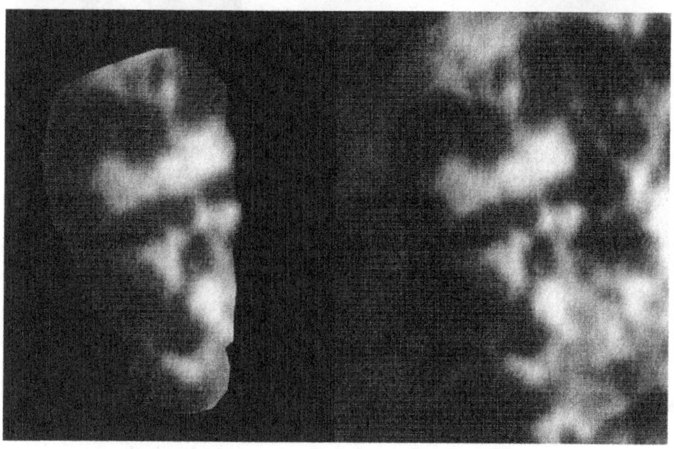

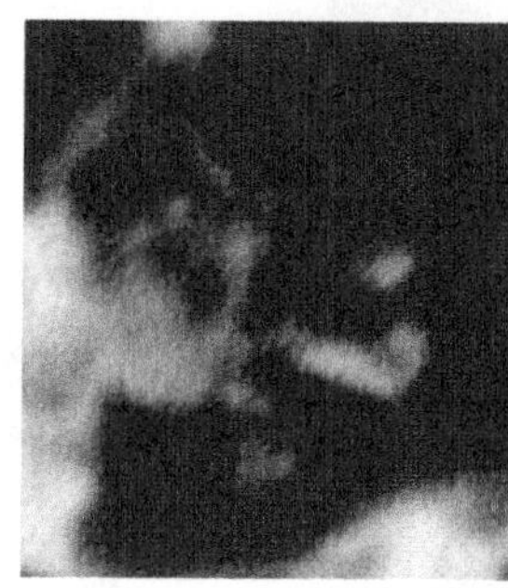

Above: Old man or "scientist".
Below: Craggy-featured monster or being.

Above: Sinister face.
Below: Bird monster face from front.

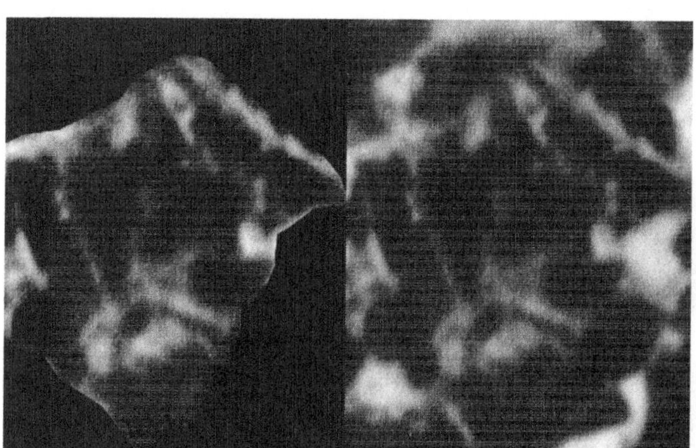

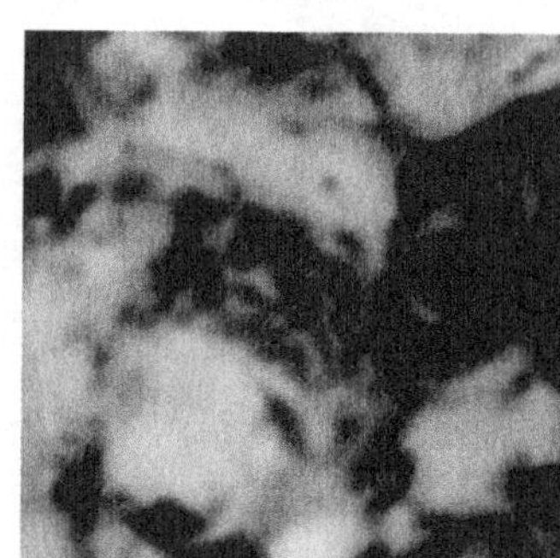

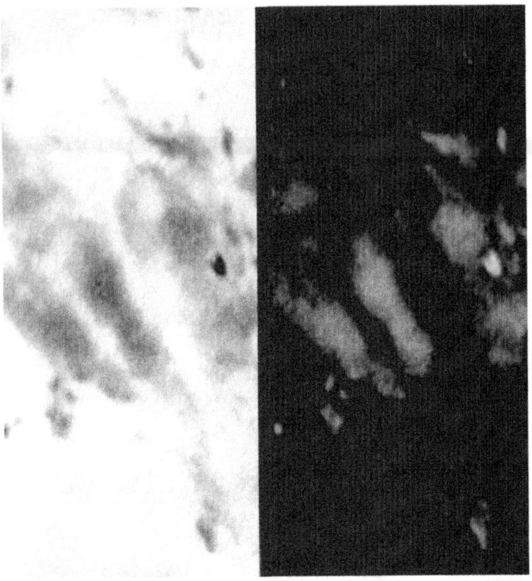

Right: Two weird faces.
Left: Nude female legs and torso.

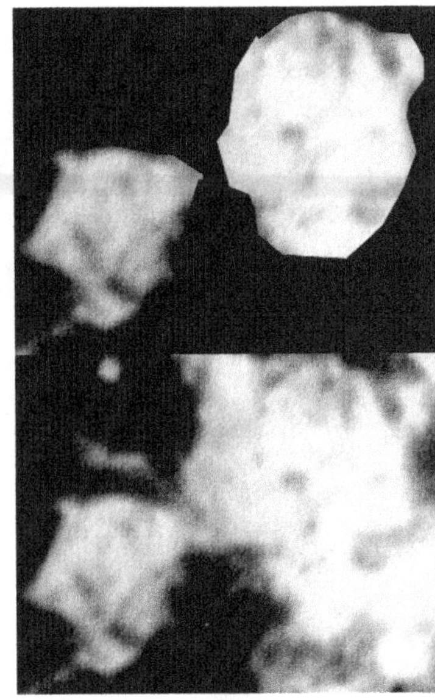

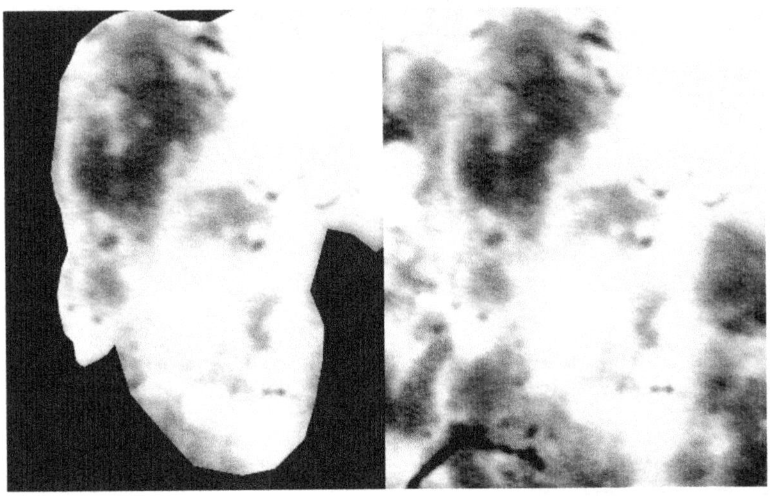

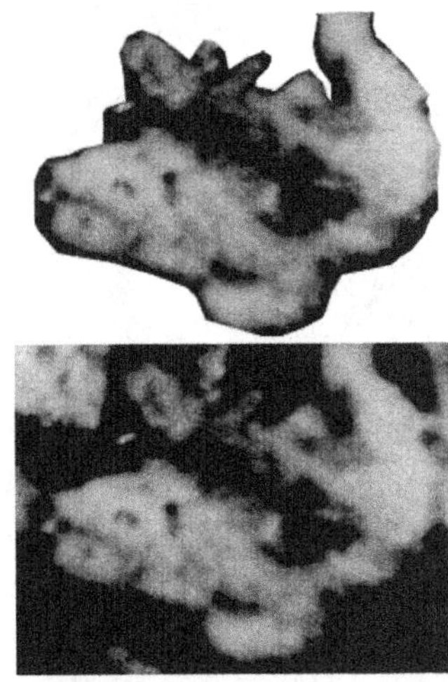

Above Left: Half-face of a man. Does this look suspiciously like Richard Shaver himself?
Above Right: Reptilian form.

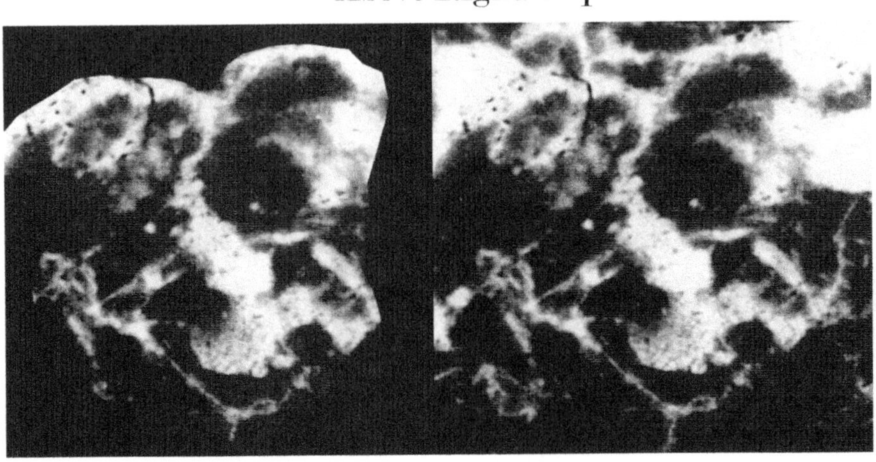

Left: Comical craggy "goblin" face.

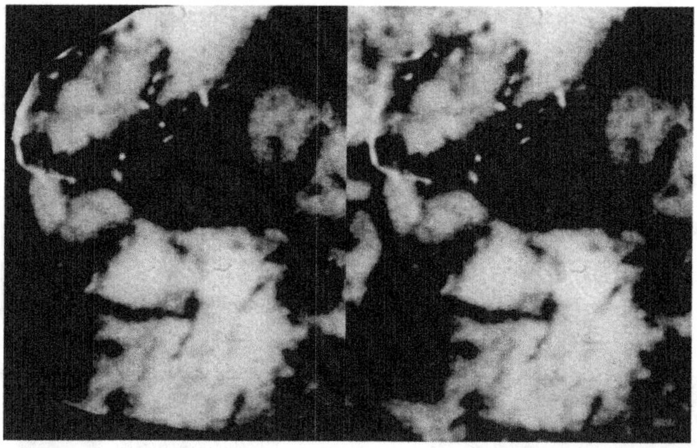

Left: Smiling tough-guy with cap pulled low.

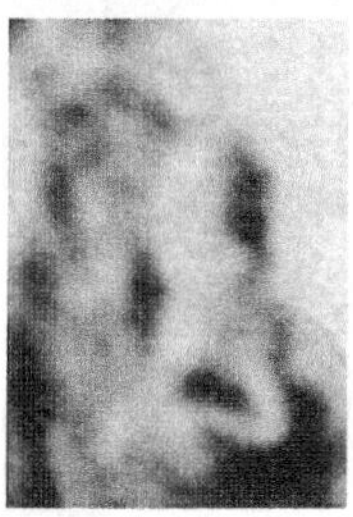

Right: Tiny face, flanked by larger "kissing" forms. See Shaver's third image description from the SEARCH article in the previous section.
Left: Leaping figure.

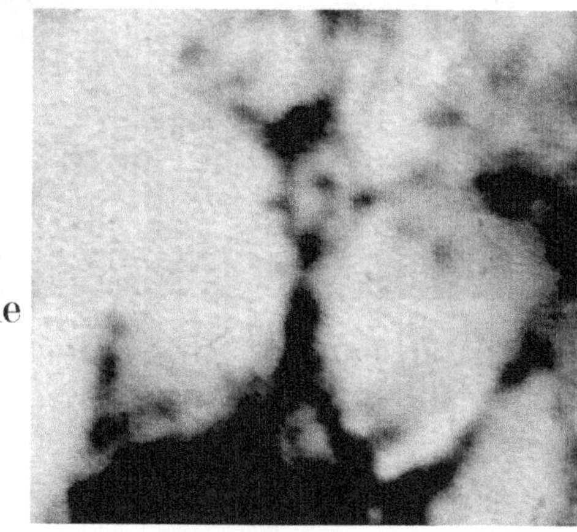

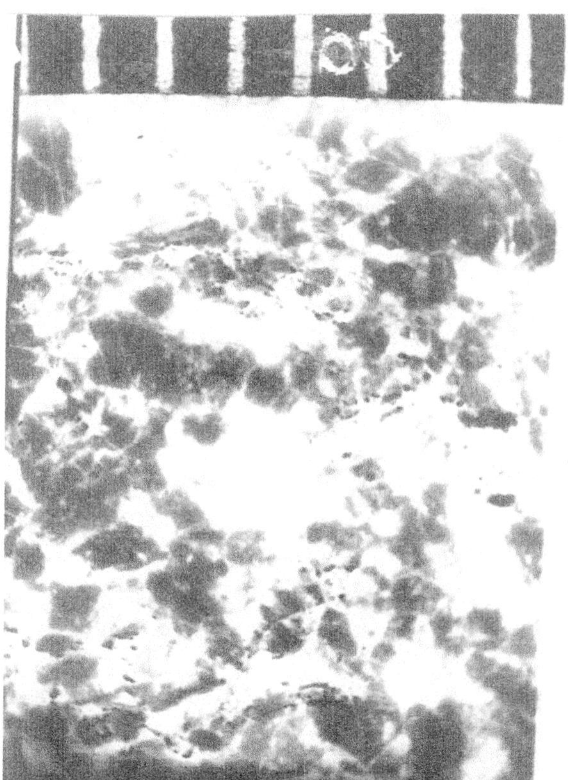

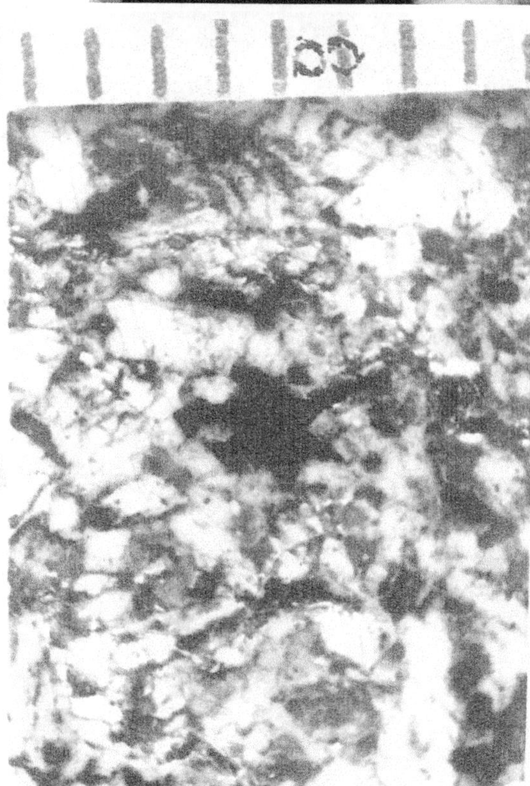

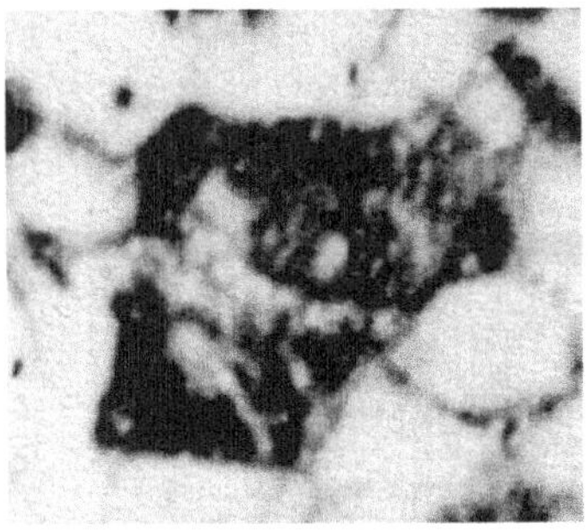

Left: An eerie, large eyed, jowled profile peers from the rock.
Right: Another bug-eyed "peeper" looks out through a hole in the rock.

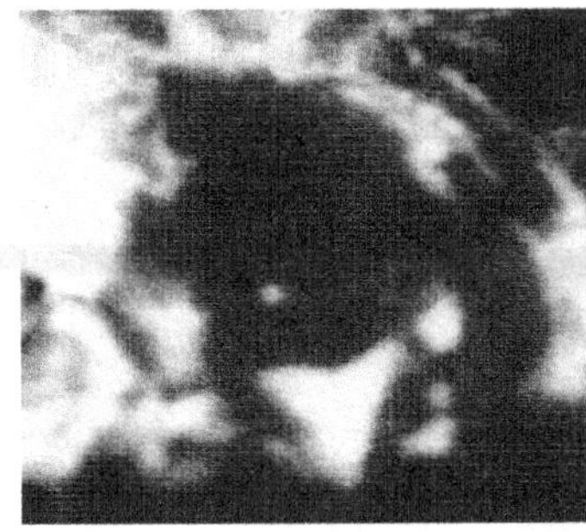

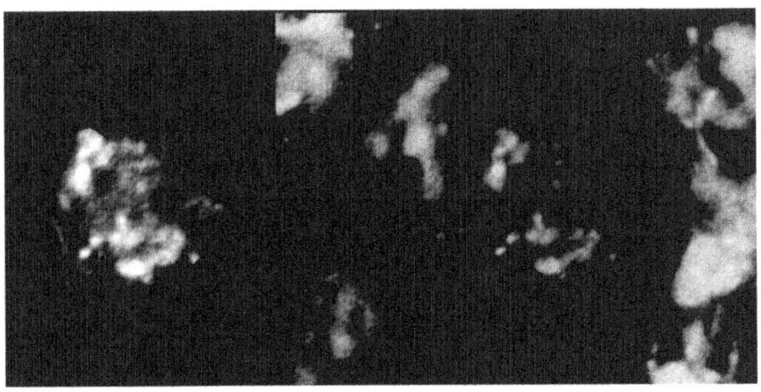

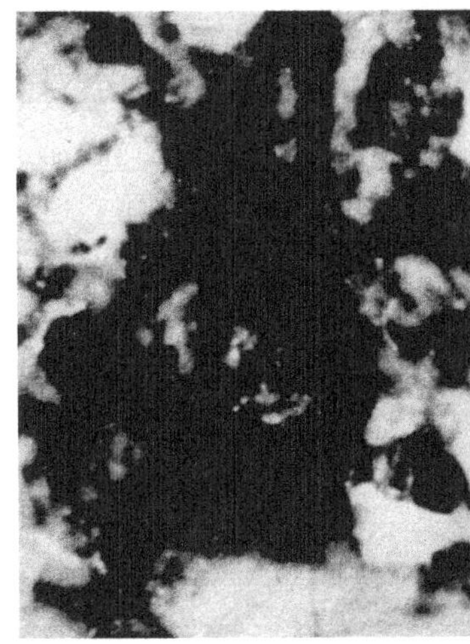

Above and Right: A "dero face" grinning from a cavern-like space.

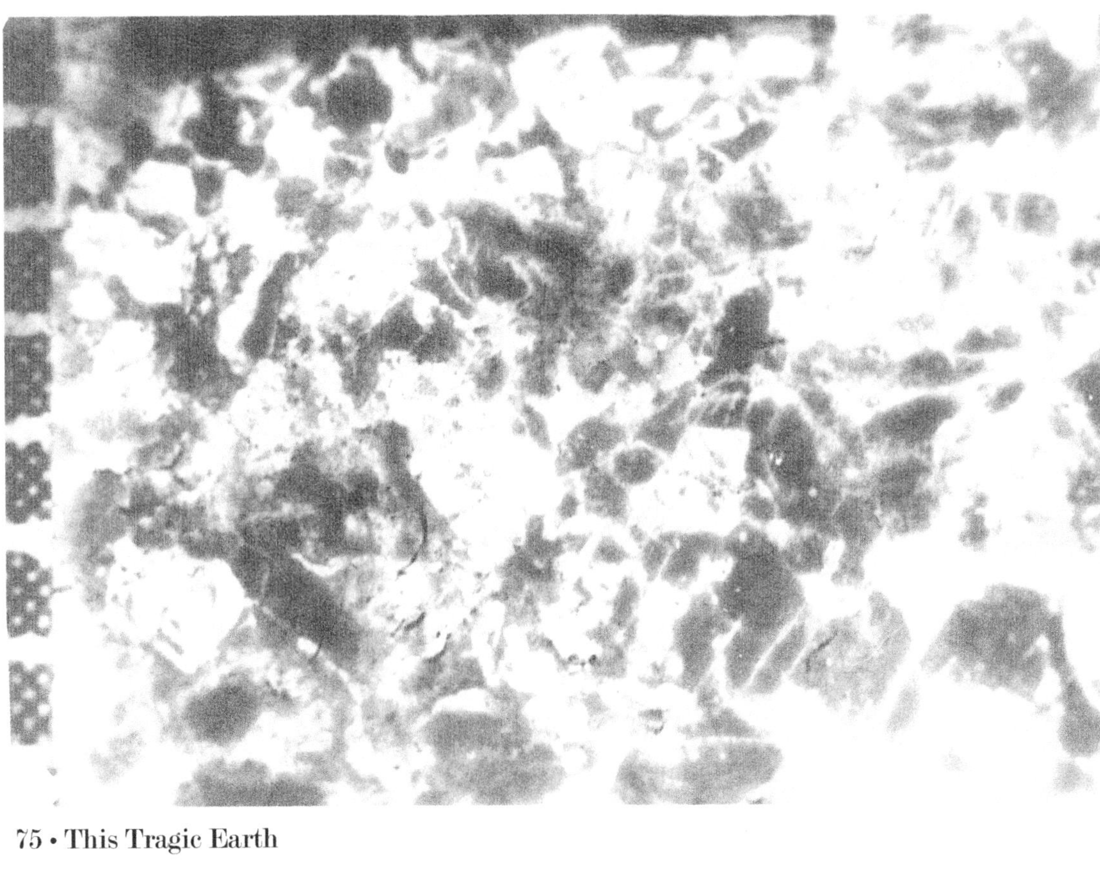

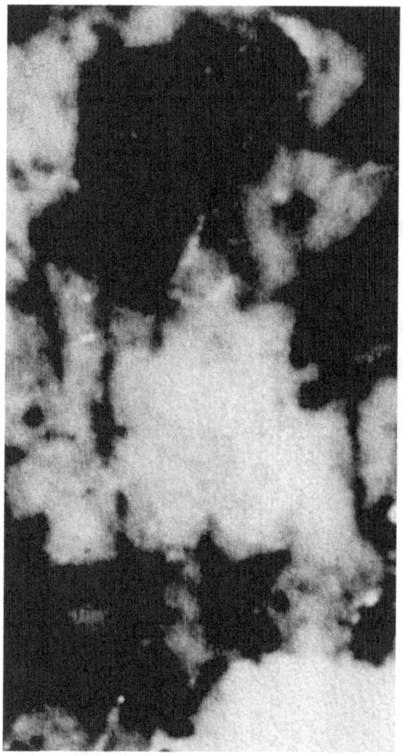

Above A topless woman, torso, shoulders, neck, head/face, and hair.

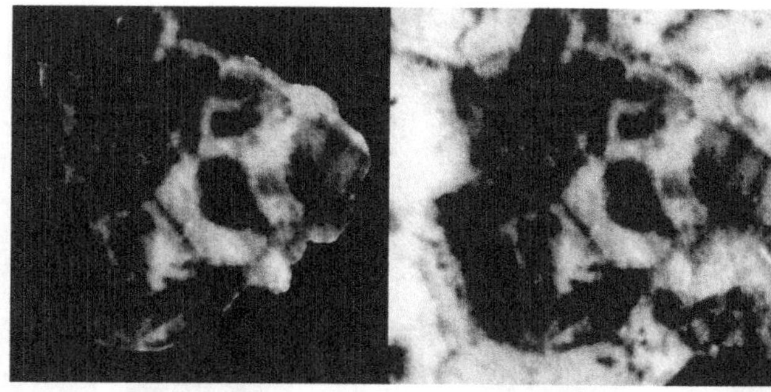

Above: Cat-Dog-Creature head.
Below: Little faces peer from the dark.

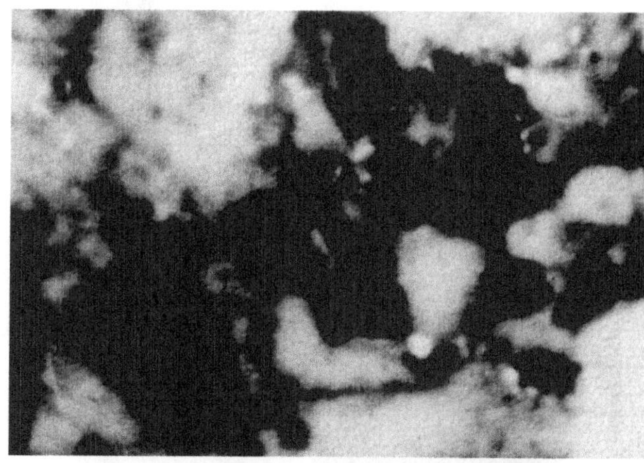

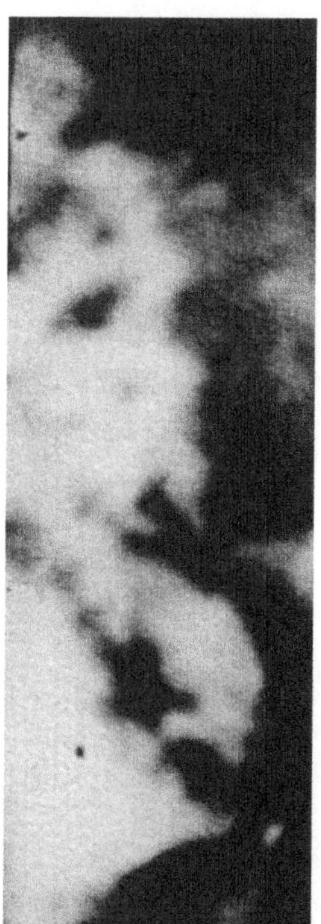

Right: A little dero/demonic figure crouches in a hole.
Left: Strange three quarter profile.

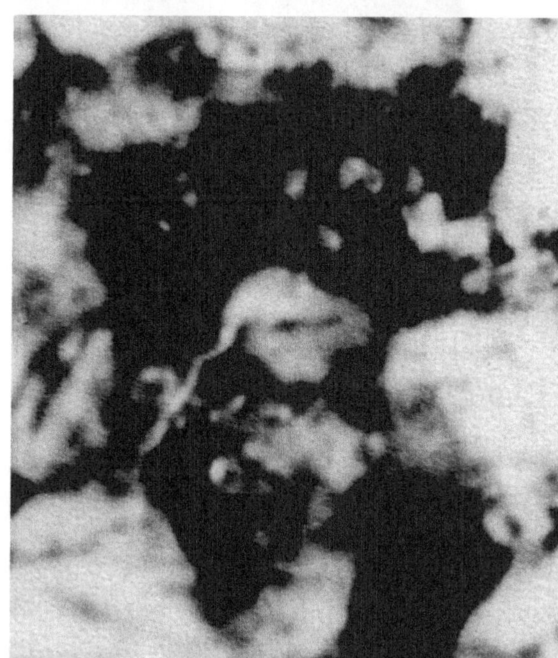

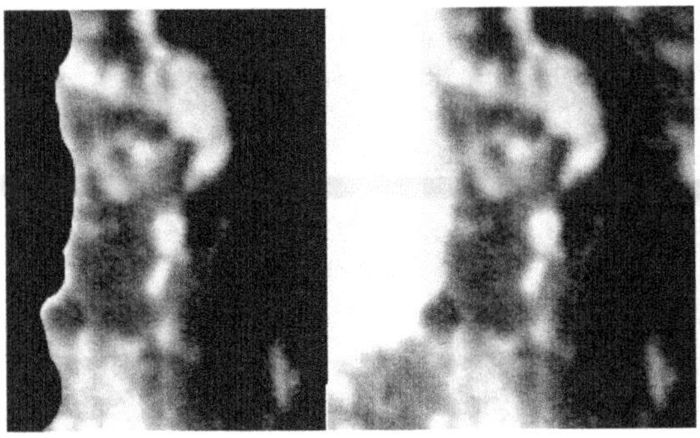

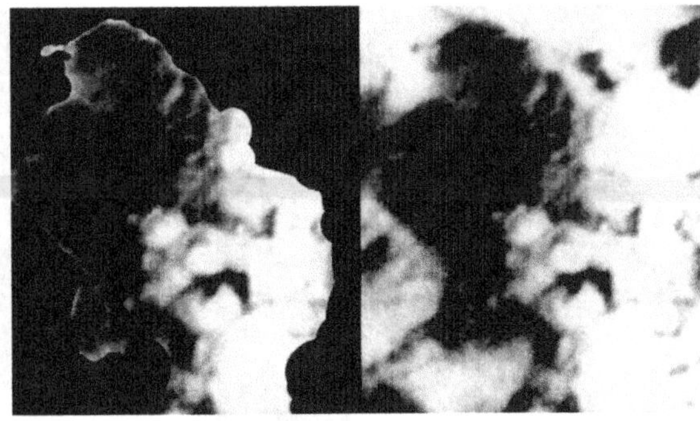

Above Right: Pensive, dark horned figure, and puffy face in foreground.
Above Left: Helmeted head/ figure.

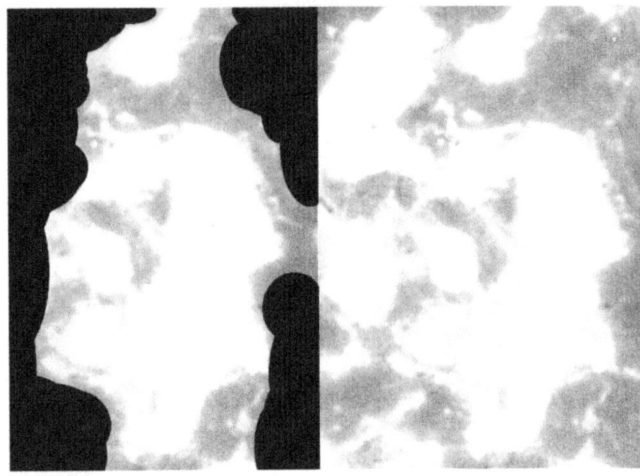

Above: "Incan" looking man, bundled in thick clothing.

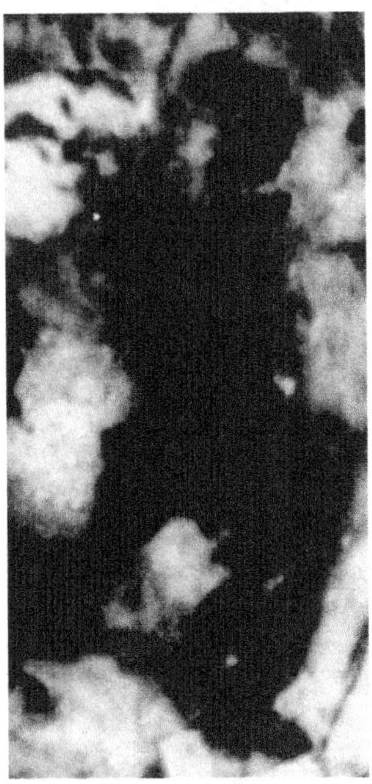

Above: Running female figure.
Right: A battle or sacrifice scene, with a muscular figure (Amazon?) at top and smaller figures throughout.

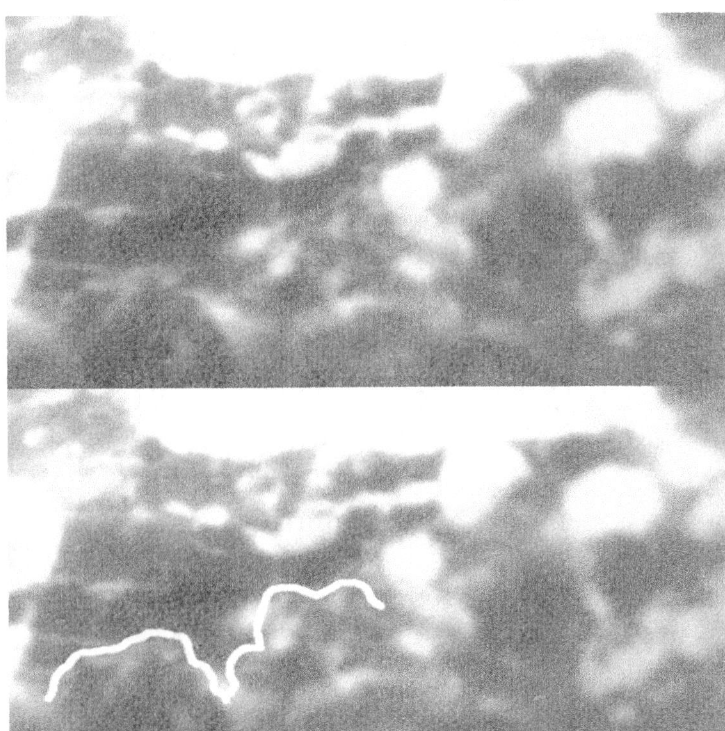

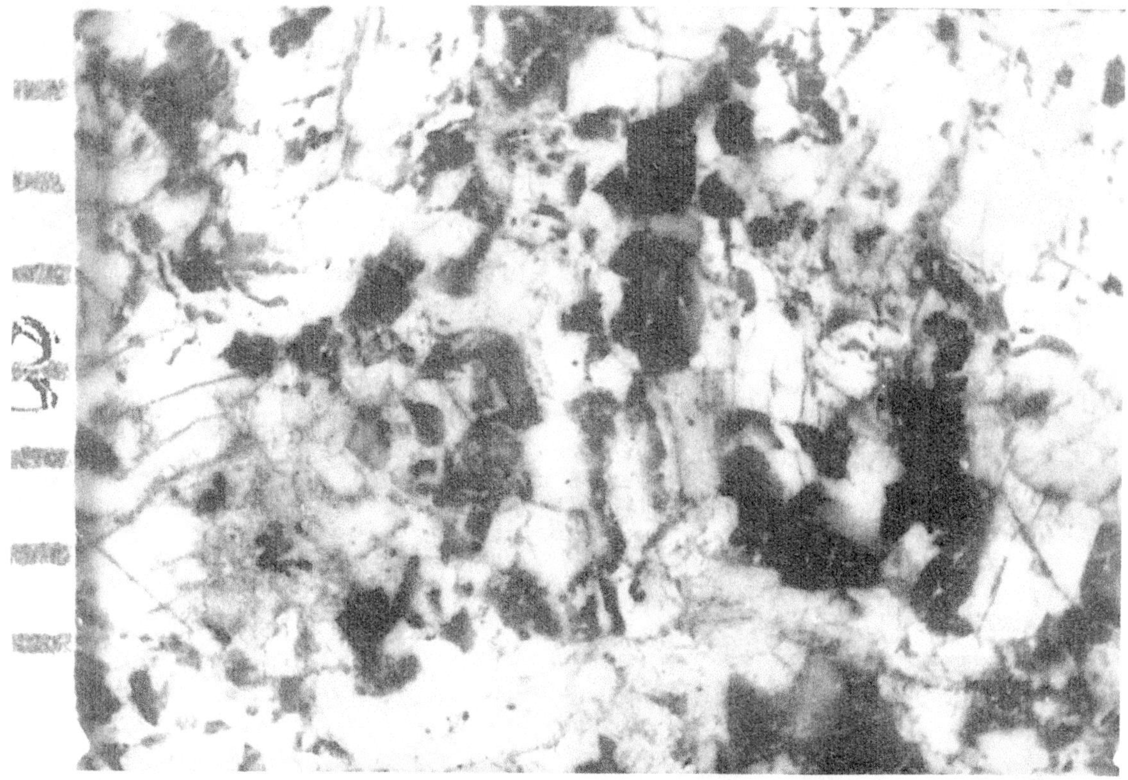

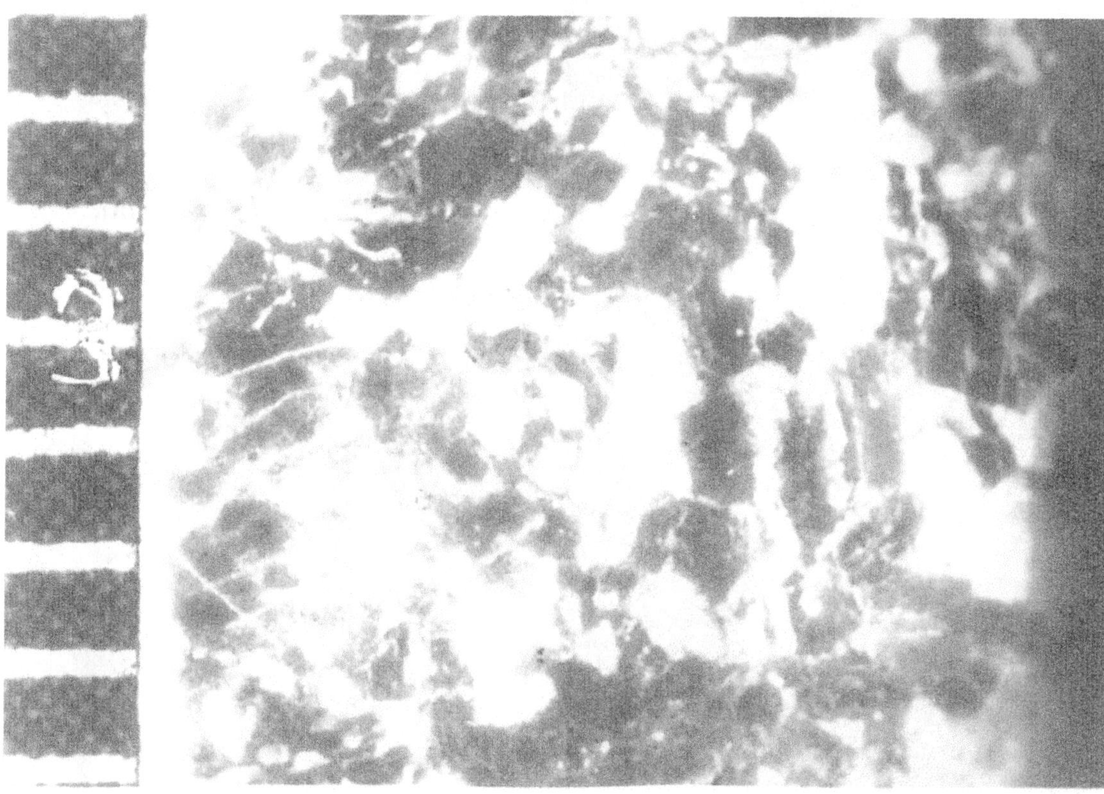

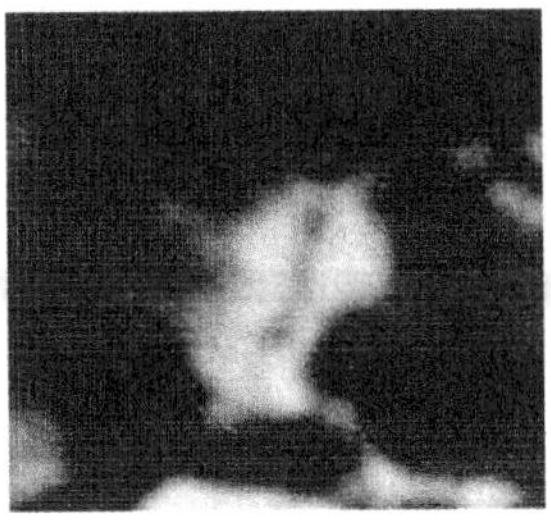

Above: Smiling profile in shadow.

Right: Reclining or hanging figure, with bent knees at top of picture.
Left Craggy profile.

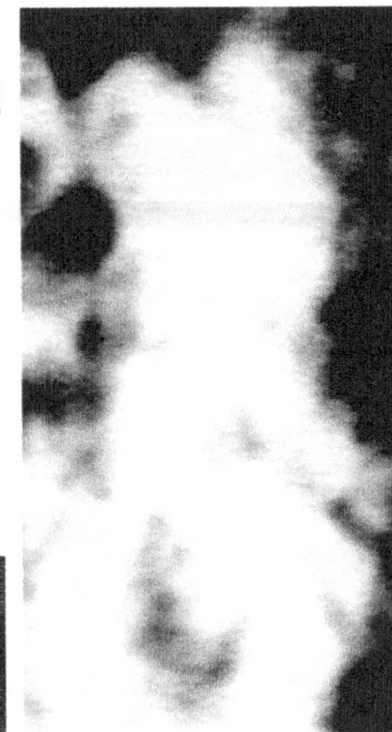

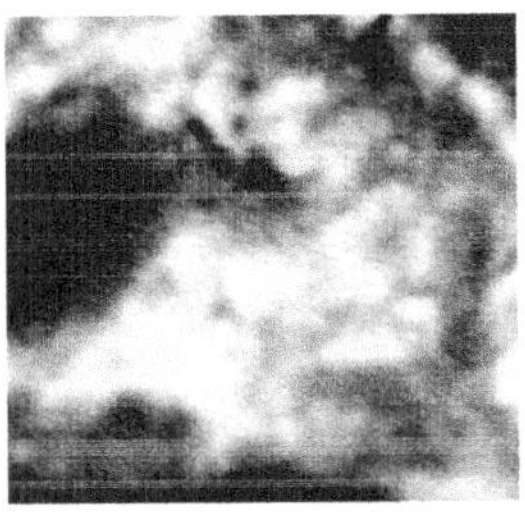

Right: Horned three-quarter profile.
Left: Monster profile.

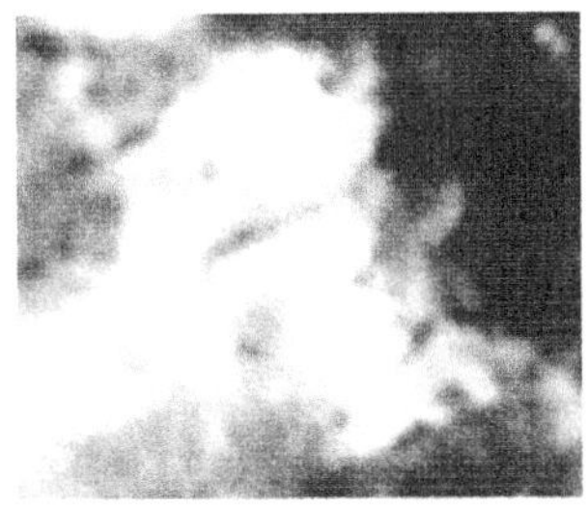

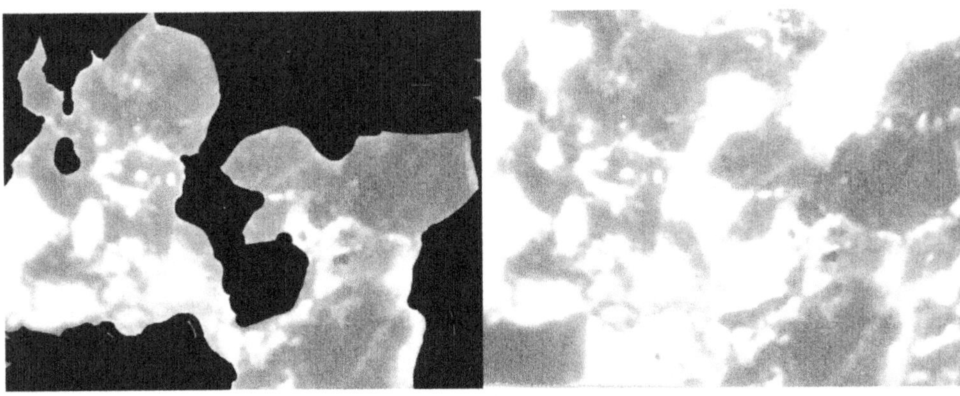

Above: Two strange masked faces in turban and tri-corner hat.
Below: Strange clustered faces.

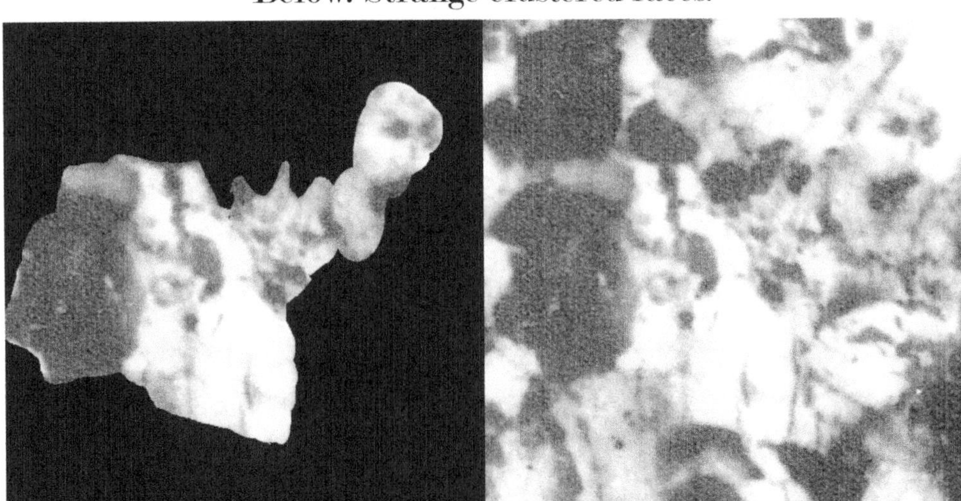

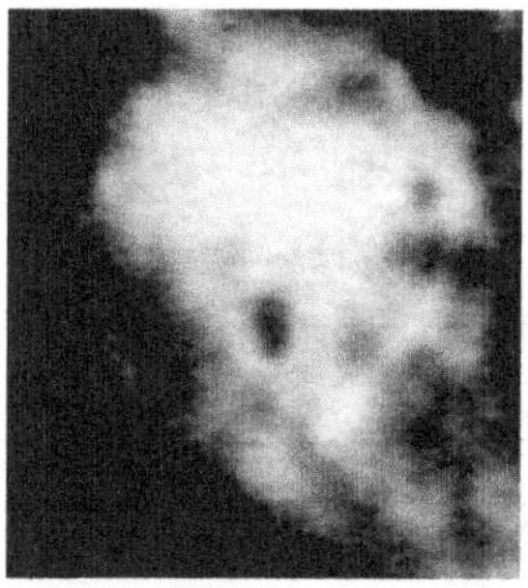

Right Cube-like robot with arms. Left: Bald man profile.

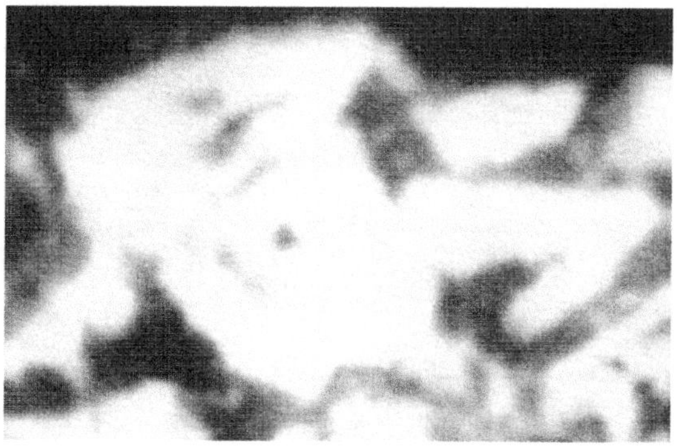

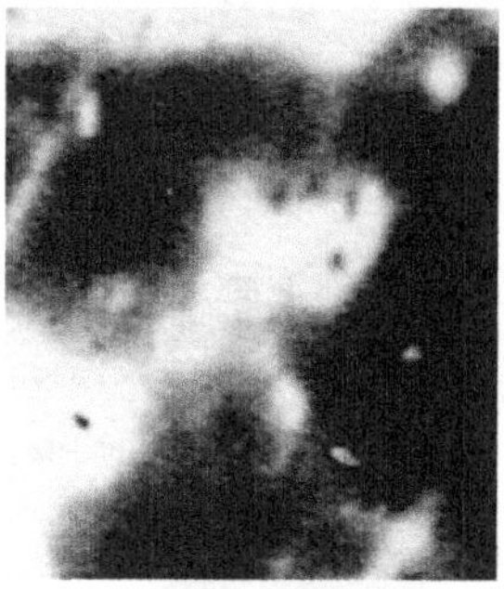

Left: Smiling and reclining Incan/Aztec/ Atlan Man. Below: Fish-man face from front.

Above: Ecto-morphic head/ face . Below: Weird profile with tongue.

Above: Dog-like head. and neck, in shadows. Below: Helmet or mask-like form.

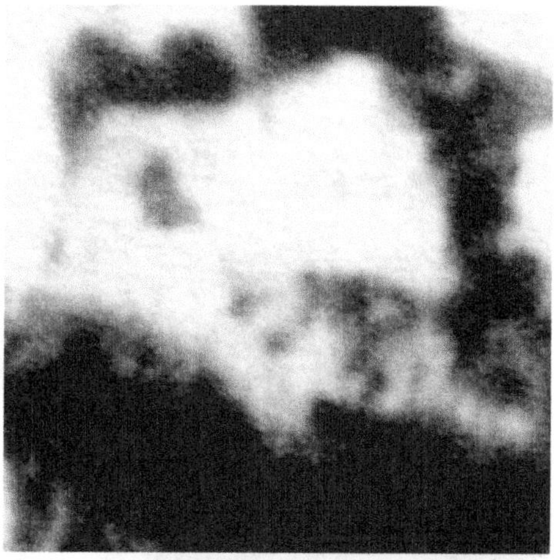

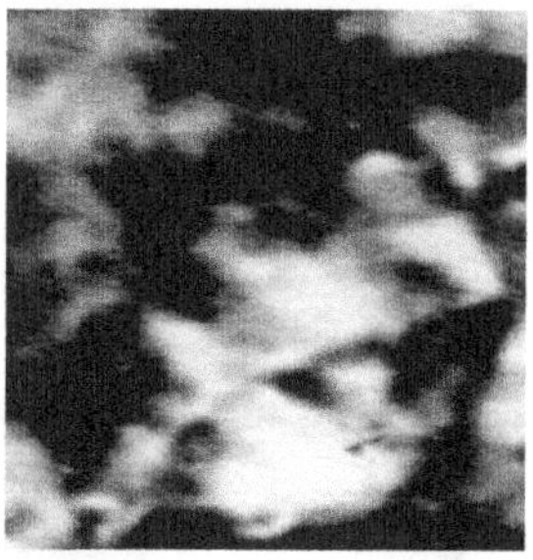

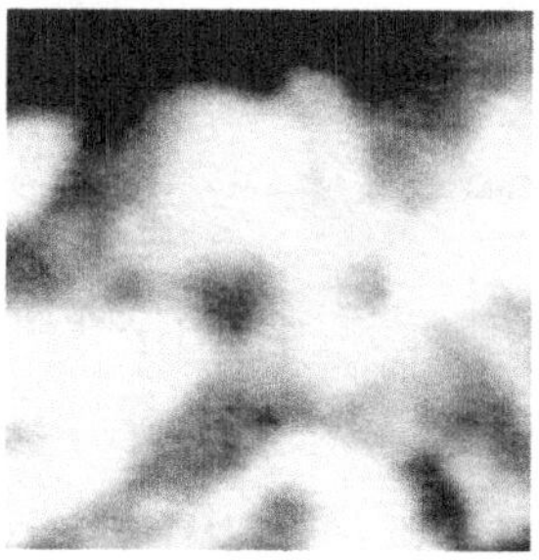

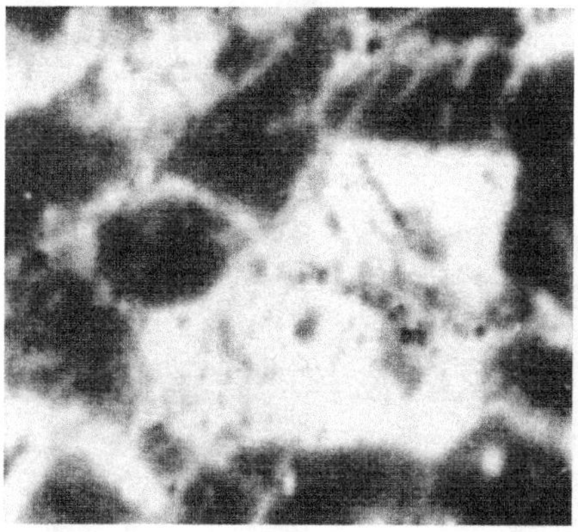

Right: Unusual "artifact-like" forms. Left: Large-nosed face.

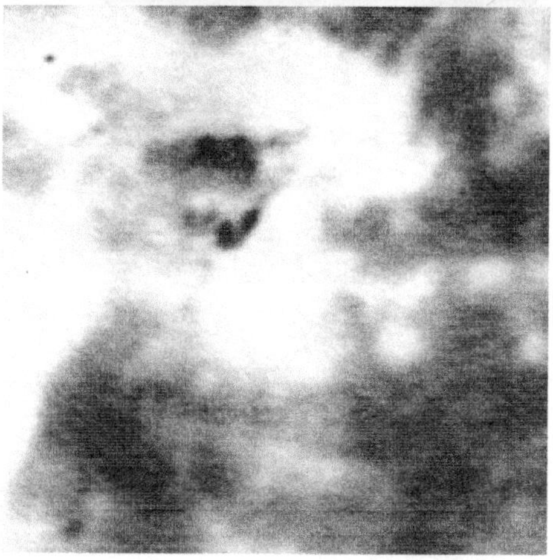

Right: "Forked tongue" skull and face profile, merged.
Below: A mask covering the top of a face and head, bottom of the face showing beneath.

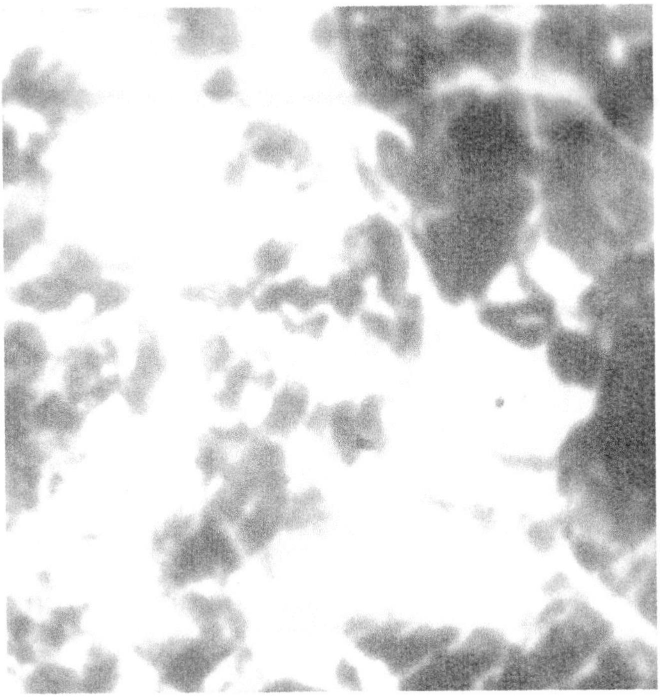

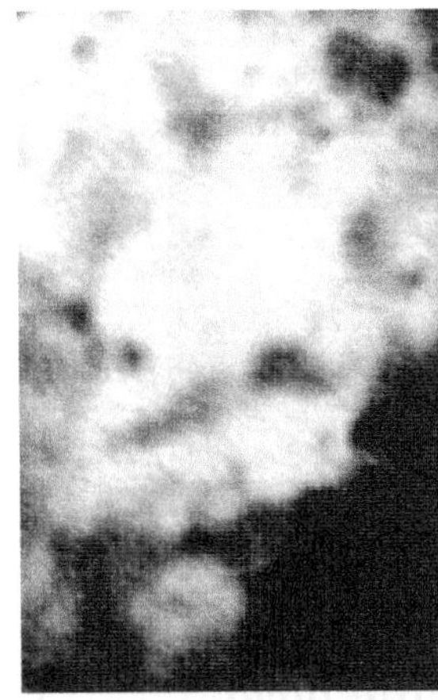

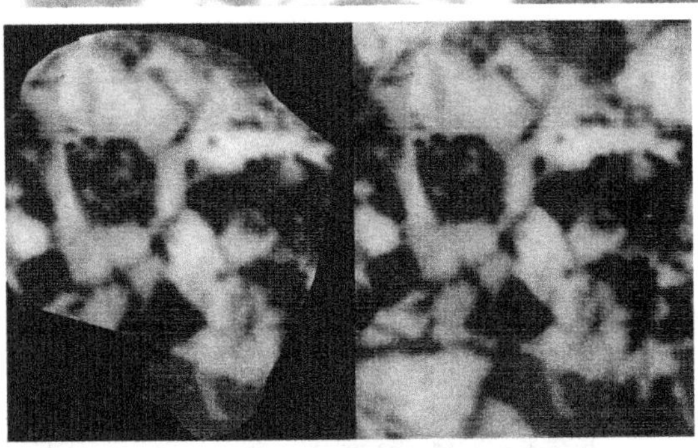

Right: Cluster of faces/ masks.

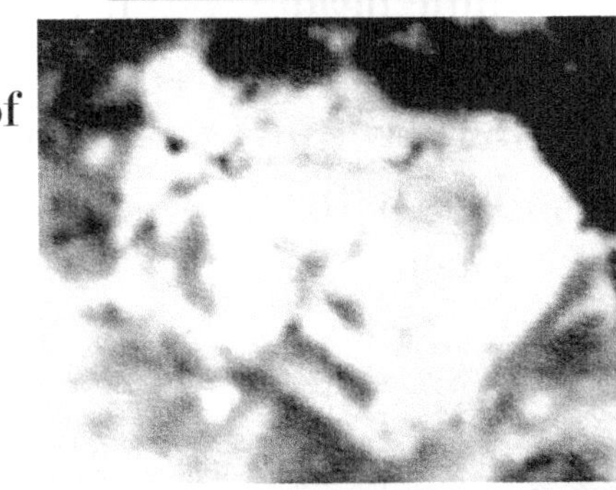

Above: Stone-like head/face.
Below: Human-animal hybrid.

Right: Big-eared "elf" profile.

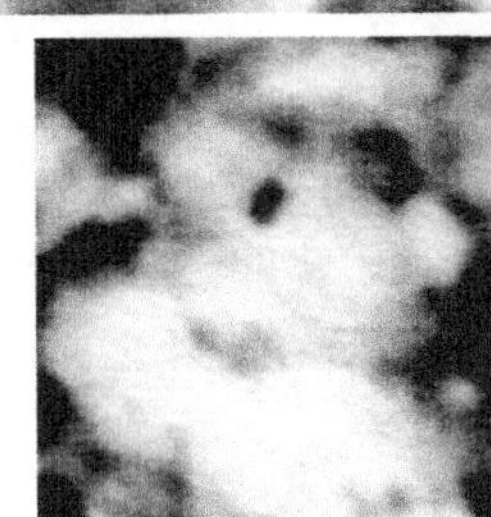

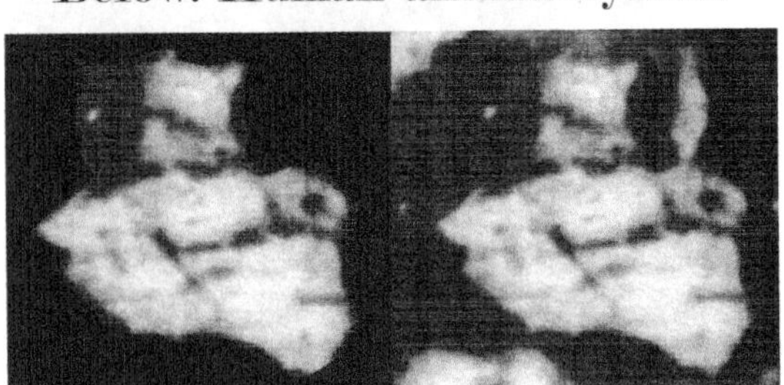

Below: Ovoid head.

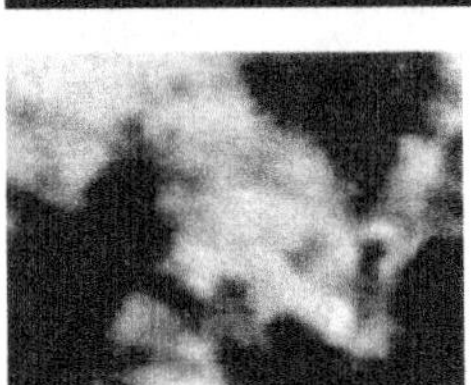

Left: Lion or hyena head.
Right: Dero or being head in cave or hole.

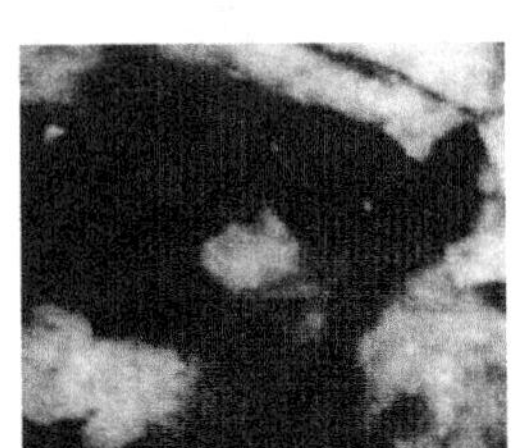

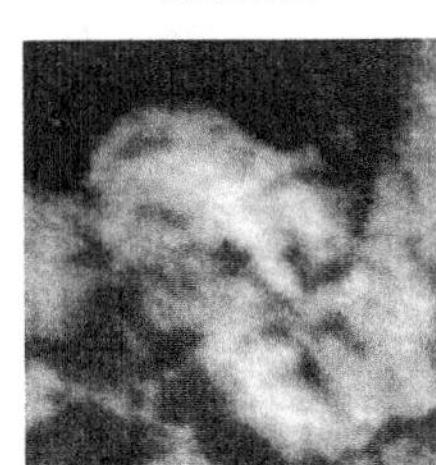

CORRESPONDENCE, WRITINGS, AND MISCELLANEA

AN INSIGHT INTO THE THEMES FOUND IN THE ARTWORK OF RICHARD S. SHAVER

RICHARD S. SHAVER ON ABSTRACT ART

I was just studying some thunder eggs on the desk here, and when I got up I passed some Picassos in an old TIME (magazine) tear of Piccasso prints in small size and as the light struck them on a slant giving not a picture but a black and white outline ..i was struck by the fact that Picasso abstracts are precisely the same sort of pattern one finds in magnifying thunder eggs ..the little jig saws that look like miniaturization bread-board hook ups... painted transistor circuits... and I wondered if you had noticed this about abstract art..it is so often the same thing as a print of rock photo ... do you like spaghetti? I'll take a side dish of Picasso

The Nude Descending the Staircase is precisely like so many rock prints . . . like somebody ran a diamond saw through her

I always thought Picasso had mind-radio robot and his paintings bear me out in this..they have to be the same sort of nut behind them.

All our artists have sabotaged minds ..and the best are the worst thisaway -thatawayand the best are the worst thisaway thataway

I feel a draft between the ears myself

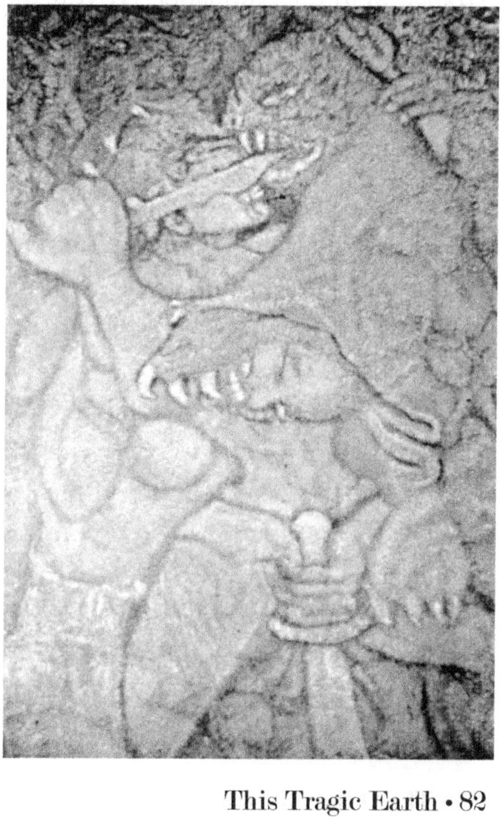

RIGHT: ONE OF SHAVER 'S PAINTINGS BASED ON ROGFOGO/ROKFOTO IMAGERY, OF A BATTLE BETWEEN AN ANTEDILUVIAN AMAZON AND AN "APE-BAT". FROM THE BOOK HE CREATED WITH RAY PALMER, *THE SECRET WORLD* (1975).

LETTER FROM RAY PALMER TO READERS OF THE OCTOBER, 1955 ISSUE OF *MYSTIC* MAGAZINE, PROMOTING "THE SHAVER MYSTERY".

Editor's Note: Original typographical errors are intact in this section.

Hello:

I am enclosing a free copy of the October 1955 issue of MYSTIC Magazine. I'd like to have you read it. Primarily because it contains the first article on the Shaver Mystery which is intended to remove the smokescreen that has covered it for more than ten years. The articles in MYSTIC are going to tell the whole truth, without any fiction added, about the strange experiences, and the strange information given by Richard S. Shaver concerning his "caves" and the people who live in them.

The fact that you are getting this letter means your name is on file somewhere in relation either to Shaver or OTHER WORLDS, and thus you aren't entirely unaware of what it's all about. But do you know that there is more to it than you think? Do you know that Shaver can back up what he says? Do you know the facts behind his original stories in AMAZING STORIES? Do you know why they were suppressed? If you like to see things "laid on the line", and a spade called a spade, that is exactly what MTSTIC intends doing. Take this October article, for instance; It is largely an introduction, giving the most important single bit of cavern lore in the Mystery, the strange Mantong Alphabet. If you were to devote a few hours to actual "sampling" of words, using the Alphabet, you'd not fail to run across some astounding things.

This letter is primarily to acquaint you if the existence (if you don't already know) of MYSTIC Magazine, and its new presentation of the Shaver Mystery. But we want to tell you that MYSTIC deals with other subjects also, and in great variety. Nowhere in the world is a magazine quite like it published. You might possibly find it interesting in more ways than one. Become one of our subscribers, or at least buy MYSTIC at your newsstand. If you don't find it the most interesting and valuable magazine you ever bought, and aren't 100% satisfied that your money was well spent, we'll refund the whole amount at any time you ask for it. This isn't a money-making project, because we don't make any money at it. Not enough people are real thinkers, and have a sufficiently open mind to back us to that extent. And we don't care. We think what we have to say in MYSTIC is important, and we will say it!

Fill in the coupon below and we'll start your subscription with the January and March 1956 issues (with the second and third Shaver articles in them, entitled: "The Rescue of Atlantis and Lemuria by the Flying Saucers" and "Why Do We Die. The Original Sin of Adam and Eve". If you already have them, tell us, and we'll start with May and the fourth article. Bear in mind that MYSTIC appears only every other month.

By the way, have you seen the NEW, dressed-up, large-sized OTHER WORLDS? Remember the good old days when AMAZING STORIES was such a terrific magazine? Well, OTHER WORLDS is cut to make those days look silly! We've got some of the best stories we've seen in the past 30 years. Like David V. Reed's CIRCUS IN TIME (better than his famous EMPIRE OF JEGGA!); Roger Arcot's THE TIMELESS MAN, a truly sensational 87,000 word novel; S.J. Byrne's THE METAMORPHS, which has us so excited masters as Robert Moore Williams, Don Wilcox, Hal Annas, Richard S. Shaver, Rog Phillips; and brilliant newcomers like Evelyn Martin. We're going to outdo anything we've ever done in science fiction with this new OTHER WORLDS. There's a bargain offer on the coupon that might interest you.

Your old friend,
Ray Palmer

DOCTOR SOFFICE OR DR. FELL?

by Richard S. Shaver

The trouble with medicine is that any doctor can be and often is mentally controlled by malevolent using the mind - radio. Thus you dont know, when you go into the Doctor's Office whether you are going to receive benevolent well-meaning care from the drugs and scalpels or whether you are going to get a dirty trick form the underworld of idiots malevolent. Not knowing which can be fatal or worse.

So "Doctor Soffice" is a reality, and is as often "Dr. Fell" of the kind you dont want and yet must pay for.

The same is true of Dentists, and the Dentist who pulls the wrong tooth with great pain is well known to all of us, I believe.

If you dont "believe" this, just think about acupuncture and the mechanics of which it works for a few moments. How can it be, where there is no evidence visible before your eyes of any connection between the needles and the miracles they accomplish?

So with malevolent medecine in your own benevolent doctor's office...right before your eyes your own doctor can be and often is malevolently controlled quite without his own knowledge of what is going on.

The same is true of the "science" upon which you rely to analyze your world and make it fit to live in. The scientist cannot rely upon his own eyes in his own microscope, for at any time the malevolent mind-radio can make him see what is not there, or "not see" what is there.

Neither science, nor medecine, nor dentistry, nor justice, can really exist under this condition of malevolent mind-radio, and the secrecy surrounding the whole operation of mind-radio conceals only malevolence, for why else would they hide such a thing?

I do not really want to go into the reasons behind the ancient secrecy surrounding mind-radio, nor its existence today. I do want to point out that medecine" must be entirely free of malevolence to be medecine of any use to any one. And today it is neither free nor is it medecin, as you well know if you read the papers.

What can you do about this horrible condition of mental servitude to evil domination in medecine and in justice and in "science".

You can talk about it, discuss it, study it until you understand its nature in the same way you understand your own musical radio on its shelf. Then you can get together and manufacture similar devices for anyone to use to HEAR mind-radio in operation, record it, publicize it, and so by shedding light upon the hideosity, pave the way for removal of the evil.

To talk about the "invisible empire" of mind-radio compelling people everywhere into acts of utter malevolence is all you can do perhaps. But even that is a lot more than anyone does, ordinarily. To be afraid to discuss mind-radio because of what others may think of you is to miss the whole point. Others THINK what they do in response to mind-radio compulsions is a fact of life you have to recognize in order to create an immunity to the slings and arrows of gossip and mud-slinging. If you do not recognize this fact of life, then the Dr, Soffice'es of the world are in fact a terrible threat, for you dont know enough to stay away from them.

Today we have all kinds of health insurance and hospital insurance which make it practical to have hospital fees to fit todays' inflated health budgets. But every time you USE these health insurances, you place yourself within reach of the malevolent's control of the medical men...you place yourself in the hands of unseen malevolence that can and does manipulate the MINDS of all men.

The peculiar sort of medecine associated with ACUPUNCURE is the medecine of the underworld benevolence. They can and do medical miracles by the mere insertion of needles into your skin!

Isn't that, in and of itself, sufficient proof of the reality of the invisible world of mind-radio?

There is benevolent application of the miraculous underworld city devices built before the flood...and it exists NOT ONLY in the acupuncture offices of the acupuncture specialists. It exists in the offices of our own doctors, too. Unseen and un -noticed it yet guides the hand and mind of many doctors in their most delicate operations. It is not an enemy nor is it malevolent.

Neither is it all-powerful God. It is the Under-People doing what they have always done, helping us of the surface.

BUT we do have the malevolent usages of the same powers of mind-radio and invisible vision beams for blood-less surgery. How to stay away from its harm is something we have to talk about and to know about, openly and generally.

THE SHAVER PAPERS

From *ALIEN CRITIC #9*, 1974

Richard S. Shaver became well known in the 1940's as the author of the Shaver Mystery. When Ray Palmer was editor of AMAZING and FANTASTIC in those pulp days, he hyped the circulation of the magazines up to 250,000 per issue by exploiting Richard Shaver's beliefs that a degraded remnant of a past super-race from the starts had once lived on Earth. Still lived in vast secret caves beneath the surface, and used ancient mind machines to influence humans to evil ways.

These dregs were called deros... And the audience for this theory were what is call the Lunatic Fringe. And Ray Palmer printed dozens of letters from people claiming to have explored caves and come across deros and terrible machines....

Science fiction fans were generally outraged by this perversion of their genre, and the derision heaped upon the once proud AMAZING and FANTASTIC....

It was later admitted/charged that Ray Palmer had himself written or rewritten most of the Shaver Mystery stories.

Eventually, the Shaver Mystery ran out of gas and faded...as did the Palmer magazines' circulations. Ray Palmer left as editor. The pulp era ended. Richard Shaver dropped from sight.

A few months ago I read in a fan magazine that Richard Shaver was alive and well in Summit, Arkansas, selling rocks.

I sent him a copy of IAC #7. He responded with a letter and some photos of cross -sections of rocks..with the claim that the ancient race had recorded vast amounts of information and visuals into what appear to be common rocks.

TO me the "pictures" were like ink blots and tea leaves and cloud formations -- you see what you want to see, and if you look long enough you'll find shapes and images that "prove" what you need to believe.

I said as much to Mr. Shaver...and mentioned that some fans thought him as mad as a hatter.

He responded with more letters and rock photos. Yet I still cound not --and still cannot --make out the images he sees so clearly.

He is frustrated, bitter, angry, discouraged.

I told him I would print passages from his letters to give him a hearing and if the readers wanted to respond fine.

Here, then, is Richard S. Shaver:

"This all happens to be true, you know. It isn't fiction. But you have to write it as fiction because the duped, ignorant publishers don't know enough to accept it as fact.

"If it wasn't true you'd go back to snail-breaking and enjoying your morning coffee. But with the imminent collapse of all society into the ruin of degradation and utter zombi-ism there is no choice, one must find a way to warn them, however mad it seems.

"From every radio there is emitted a vibration of quite paralyzing potency, disguised as the latest rock sound. It paralyzes their poor minds, and makes them willing suckers for every fool sales scheme designed to overcome their poor, staggering incomes.

"You know you have always wondered what and why was rock music? All at once it strikes you...it's part of the enemy invasion, and in their tunnels underground they creep on and across the land...inserting their sound tentacles into every home.

"Snail-breaking no more, you pound away at the enemy keys of the confounded typewriter, confounded enemy legs and arms sprouting from under its carriage. It is evilperson everywhere taking over the world. Ah, geez, it's awful.

"Then you remember...it all happened long ago and what the people and yourself are...is the residue, the aftermath of the take-over, the poor spineless recipients of the pottage left by those who took it all long ago.

***

"It is pitiful and horrible, but you must not listen, there is still one sprout on the Tree of Ygdrasil and we must remove the worms from it and let it grow."

***

"Ygdrasil was once, like the Chestnut, a great tree reaching everywhere through all space...the man-tree, with the fruits of all his genius flowering on every planet through all the long marches of sunlight and dark and emptiness and shadows and holes in the planetoids.

"Oh well, Ygdrasil is long dead and man is but a remnant of diseased, ignorant flith on this one small ball of dung...what can it matter what one does or does not do?

***

"Will Richard Nixon join his brother bag-man VP Agnew...in degradion and the slime of the back alley apartment?

"It's all a ruse to deploy the enemy ranks behind the diversion, that's what it is. Nixon is a telaug puppet pulled two ways, both wrong.

"Maybe one should look at it differently, as a battle of firid lost then thousand years ago to the enemy. Then one could have the results of the world-take-over in plain view, with everyone knowing they are slaves to the secretive mind-controlling vibrations from underground but unable to wiggle a toe except as the great overlay field commands. Nobody can tell Nixon, why tell anyone?"

***

"The madmind of RSS slaves away, still warning future man of his imminent demise in the far past, or was it tomorrow yesterday?"

***

"I'd rather than man than a modern stf-fan who swallows the stuff they call sci-fic today and thinks he is getting the best. I'd rather be mad...never mind. You know the mad business started the same place the rumor that Raymond A. Palmer wrote Shaver (stories)...in false name letters put out by a few fen by the thousands.

"There was so much of this that Palmer asked me about it and showed me some bearing on my own signature supposed to be by me...it's no wonder they think I'm mad...they signed my name to enough nutty letters.

"There was even a fan who got a girl pregnant using my name...and she came to the AMAZING office looking for me...until Palmer showed her my picture and she realized she'd been had.

"I always wondered what I would have done if she hadn't been able to distinguish the difference...if the guy had looked like me too.

"So I'm mad. It's a matter of degree...I read Ted White and think the same thing about the whole field...it's no wonder I quit writing. I enjoyed life a lot more than slaving over potboilers...who wants it...raising pigs is a better go.

"Comparing the SANE go with my own...I can enjoy a tree or a deer or a dog... and the sane cant'. They have to think some stereo-type think inherited from generations of madness. They have to shoot the deer, cut the tree, and rebuff the dog. In that way I am the reverse of average... I worship the tree, stand in awe of the deer's grace...caress the dog.

"I remember my dogs better than my wives in their graves...Which is perhaps mad. Who am I to say what is sane, I'm mad.

"I dream about dogs long gone in their graves. Other people dream about other things I suspect. I am anything but average.

"I use to have a dog like a wind hound...who would leave the ground thirty feet from me to light on my chest...and if you think you can forget that kind of love you never had it."

***

"I like it that way, believe me. It's the fen who are mad.

***

"...with guys like you standing bumbly dumb in the way with their idea that dero don't exist and the telang is imaginary. The telaung is no more imaginary than the common radio and there are just as many of them in use.. but secret to the common herd.

"I try to do something about that...to tell them they are being had... and try to rescue an ancient library of rock books from the ignorance that makes road gravel out of all surface rock..."

***

"The mad angle is strictly a product of dero mind tamper on the common herd... and little I can do against a world full of zombies listening to the secret radio they think is their thought."

***

"Rock books are our best path to the future that you think is being described thru sci-fic wonder stories. It ain't. Rock books are genuine science...quite ignored by the starry-eyed fen who think Shaver is mad.

"Rock books are real and contain space data is a fact...how to tell the stumble dumb is the problem. they can't get it thought them long enough to really look at a few rocks for themselves."

***

"Photos of pre-flood residents are quite available and quite detailed...but you don't 'interpret' them...you study them for details. Nobody interprets a rock book until he has studied many thousands of them and learned something."

***

"Rock books are an immense loom of the whole science of the Atlantean culture of vast magnitude. On the horizons of man's future it is his whole future... or none at all if handled in the brusque idiotic way it's been handled to date."

***

"Rock books can look mad, too, but they ain't, either. They just need the right optics to reveal themselves...and the 2mm scan isn't easy with ordinary cameras... you get too many planes of view with too many 2mm areas scrambled together."

"Such photos of sliced rock book can provide remarkable portraits of people and things like gadgets...with simple photography. But getting down to 4 to 8x on 35mm takes a bit of getting use to close-up processes...and knowing what you got when you got it requires some more work in the darkroom...and it is this work I was requesting, not opinions. Just find me some guy stained fingers who also has a brain..."

***

"The problem is in understanding that they (rock books) are...like holograms...a product of a different method of photography and of the printing of pictures in solids...and cannot be in any way judged or understood by trying to analyze them upon the basis of your own mental frame of reference based upon 2-do pictorials in news-zines and magazines."

***

"Reason I want you and those in your position of contact with fandom is the cost of hologram devices...I can't afford them. Some of them can and should on this particular problem because of the contents.. which WILL yield some sense to persistent photography of the ordinary 2-di sort...and WOULD yield the whole system of scan holography to some persistence with the same devices... and that is what I was asking...to try to interest somebody who could afford it on the possibilities...."

ROCK HOUSE STUDIO
Richard S. Shaver
Summit, Arkansas 72677

HIDEOSITIES

by Richard S. Shaver
Written circa 1969

Some things other than light need to be hidden beneath bushels, while many lights that are not hidden under baskets should perhaps be extinguished. It isn't necessary to string a lot of words together in meanings that are not anything but more words strung upon our overburdened necks already arched with the outpourings of the radio, TV and "News Conferences."

What is necessary is a way, a real light in the darkness, instead of which we get misinformation ad infinitum and with embellishments of cliches that were worn out when Noah was hammering on his ark.

Hideosities is a necessary peek at the hidden whispering, the endless cruelty of the unspoken, the awful darkness of the lack of mind now pregnant on our horizon of unwanted things. You won't like Hideosities, and you aren't supposed to know they exist (especially by those who ARE hideous, cruel, unthinking agents of the darkness itself). They're there, these agents of darkness, spread out across the world with their black wings fluttering to hide all truth and all goodness forevermore. But somehow they are visible even in the darkness we call "modern knowledge" (and other words like "technology"; always remembering that "technology" in Japan means Mercury poisoning in the villagers' fish, and in the USA means dead birds on the oil-covered beaches).

The black wings of their reaching, hiding thought are active in every single mind on earth...obscuring all truth and all wisdom with a blanket of "invisible" thought waves sent out from vast and ancient underground installations of telaugmentive stations...and to live we have to learn it, and learn to do something about it besides whisper in the darkness of ignorance.

To live again, man whispers, watching the darkness descend again upon the "new" world of hope he has been so busily erecting these past two centuries. The new dark age of modernity has some very hideous markings upon its facade of glittering ambiguity and noble aspirations toward utter lack of mind. It is easy to throw mud at it, but to understand it is something else again. It is easy to throw a leper out of the village, but to stop the infectious spread of the disease is not really that simple. The cause of modern degeneracy and the decay of our institutions has to be isolated in fact, and not just in words.

It's not so easy to tell a people lost in the ignorant darkness that is utter lack of all knowledge of their own past and their own deprivation of their own inheritance. It's not so easy to be heard in the welter of words that is really a smoke screen behind which our worst parasites operate. Everywhere this smoke screen of endless babble obscures all possibility of genuine thought...the "media" operate perpetually to obscure all real information, apparently unknowingly their worst evil is ignored and hidden by their own efforts.

The "Captive Audience" sits and watches their TeeVee, and never knows that what they watch is drawing their attention from their greatest need and their most pressing priority.

None of us really has the time to spare to be impregnated every ten minutes with soap commercials yet we are subjected to it in the name of commercialism, whatever name it goes by we can't afford that sort of mind enslavement.

I don't really care to buy a Skid-No-More tire, either. I don't think we should have any autos active anywhere, because of their ultra-poisonous by products and effect upon life. Yet I have to live with them roaring by and can't even hear my TEEVEE as it wastes my time with auto commercials.

To focus on the Hideosities of the Title of this piece, let's look at the fields of hidden thought which control this monstrosity of commercialism that lays like a blanket of mud upon the whole landscape of life.

Lift your eyes from the three wives of the soap opera, and listen for a minute to an old wisdom bird.

Tele-augmentive mind-rule exists, and consciously or unconsciously most of us have felt it, have noted there is something wrong about thinking. Something hampering us is constantly noted, but seldom spoken of. Well I am speaking.

The telaug and the telemach were once openly active all over earth, in pre-deluge times. Today they are still active, but secretly. The telaug is the device that listens to your mind's workings at a distance, and the telemach is the other device which can CAUSE you to think and act differently than you otherwise would. The meaning is "tele-make"...it makes you do things.

These are not properly science fiction concoctions, created on paper to entertain you. They are very ancient facts of life, still with us, secretly used on us. There is only one place such a thing can be mentioned seriously, and that place is in just such fanzines as this one. No "serious" publication will handle such effusions, and you cannot hear about it in any popular publication today, since Amazing declined into its present form.

I would not bother, if the motivation behind its secret use was clean and good and wholly benevolent. It is difficult enough to be heard about anything above the roar of the motors and the babble of the TV and Radio, and little enough of any real use is heard by anyone from the Media. For instance, do you realize the ONLY educational program regularly seen and heard on TV is Sesame Street? I get 5 channels on my TV, and that is it! Sesame Street is the only choice if you really feel you should learn something, and I can now count to ten and have an insatiable appetite for cookies.

I keep wondering...wondering what TV would be if it was not so helpless under the blanket of mind-rule (which, of course, we must pretend does not exists).

I am just one who got tired of pretending it wasn't there, long ago. From there on, one finds one is a controversial something or other...polite words for S.O.B. I do not want to say it's no controversy, it's a Hideosity, a blanket of smothering mindmud.

To agree with me, people find terrifically difficult, and in fact find they have to learn something about it. Since learning anything more difficult than Sesame Street's simplicities is not possible from a TV set, they don't learn enough to understand that Shaver stands for something besides controversy.

I go on, pretending always that there ARE people in the world with minds that do not want to be mind slaves. But some days this gets a bit difficult.

Today, since the advent of Alpha wave mind-wave devices, and the experimental use of such devices everywhere, the picture is a bit different, and many people are actually accepting the possibility of telaug and telemach waves.

I do really think mankind HAS to throw off this blanket, one way or another, and find out about the real world they live in, rather than accepting the surface appearances as all of life.

I really feel we should get something a bit more advanced for those of us who are out kindergarten. From TV, the Radio, and that other thing, the antiquated Newspaper. I don't feel that the immense technological accomplishment behind the TV set should be solely devoted to the phone conversations of the three wives of soap operas.

Of course, you can learn to cook from that so-sensible woman named Dinah Shore. But somehow I don't feel we are getting from TV all that we should get, do you? And if you add up all the hours you have spent watching Johnny Carson, and then subtract from that all the hours wasted, you don't seem to have a lot left on the credit side. Somehow we deserve better, I believe. In fact, I know it.

What we should be getting is construction details of mind-improving devices like the new Alpha wave devices, but far more advanced. We need better minds to cope with the decay of our world. Now, it may be that the total population really is composed of retarded children of advanced age, as the TV programs seem to be designed for the, and to still further retard their thinking.

But personally I have always felt that the total population of possible audience mind had a higher potential for learning than that. I may be wrong, and sometimes I feel that I am wrong sitting in front of Johnny Carson or Barbara in the morning.

And then I FEEL that Hideosity, shutting off the real live thinking and turning on the stupidity that we accept as the norm of life.

So I work my wits to find a way to do something about it. Which, believe you me, isn't simple. For the thing used to accomplish this vast nothingness of thought was built by super beings long and long ago...and it still works. It was NOT built to do the stupid thing it is used for today. It was built to accomplish just the reverse, and once, long ago, it accomplished its purpose. And man conquered space and moved out to the stars, and the moon left its orbit about the sun and collided with the earth and wiped out the ancient tracks of the superior race that once was US.

Today their work is used to hold us back from re-treading that path. And about all I can do about it is to talk about it, most unsuccessfully. But I try. So I keep repeating...The normal stupidity which our great TV networks use as a figure upon which to base formulas around which they design their "shows" ...is no accident. Neither is it normal. It is a present from the Underworld, and we have got to do something about it.

Man has a much higher potential than he is given credit for having. And we had better start catering to this potential, while it still exists. What can YOU do about it??? To begin with, quit wasting your time reading this kind of crap and concentrate on improving yourself by becoming a young Republican and voting for Richard Nixon ...no, that's not right.

You can entertain your own best motivations, rather than giving in to the steady hidden drive toward stupidity given off by the "secret" telemach. No, that's not right...it is like the wind and you are like a tumbleweed, without any inner drive...you have to let it roll you forever toward nowhere. Give up...let it waste all your life. written.

Below is a transcription of Shaver's legendary MANTONG Alphabet, the root of all human language (and strangely similar to Latin and Greek root words). Taken from FANTASTIC Magazine, July, 1958.

A - Animal: (Used AN for short)

B - Be: To exist (Often used as a "command")

C - Cen: To see. (C-on: to understand)

D - De: Detrimental, disintegrate energy (The second most important symbol in the alphabet)

E - Energy: (An all-pervading concept including the idea of motion)

F - Fecund: (Used "fe" as in fe-male-fecund man)

G -Generate: (Used "gen")

H - Human: (A very metaphysical concept here not fully understood but used in the sense "H-you-man": a human is an H-man)

I -Self, ego: (Same as our English)

J - Generate: (A duplication of G, but with a delicate difference in shade of meaning. Actually KA. in contrast to Ge is a very important distinction. G is the generating energy, while J is animal generation per se)

K - Kinetic: as in motion or energy

L - Life

M - Man

N - Seed: Spore (Child as "ninny")

O - Orifice: (A source concept)

P - Power:

Q- Quest: (As in quest-ion)

R-Horror: Danger (Used AR, symbol of a dangerous quantity of disintegrate force in the object)

S- Sun: (Used "sis";an important symbol, always referring to a "sun" whose energy is given off through atomic disintegration)

T - Integration Growth: (Used TE; the most important symbol of the alphabet; the true origin of the cross symbol. It signifies the integrative force of growth as, all matter is growing- the intake of gravity is the cause. The force is T. TIC means the science of growth. Integration-l-Con (understand)

U - You

V - Vital: (Used as VI; the stuff Mesmer calls" animal magnetism")

W - Will

X - Conflict: (Force lines cross each other)

Y - Why

Z - Zero: Nothing. Neutralization (A quantity of energy of T neutralized by an equal quantity of D. Futility)

Below is a transcription of "Woods","The Angel Tree--Psalm to a Maiden", and "The Hollow Hills" from the fanzine *LOKI*, Summer 1948 Here we see a rare, early glimpse of a very literary style on the part of Richard S. Shaver. This demonstrates quite plainly that he was a writer in his own right, and was capable of writing the prose so often "blamed" on Raymond A. Palmer in later years.

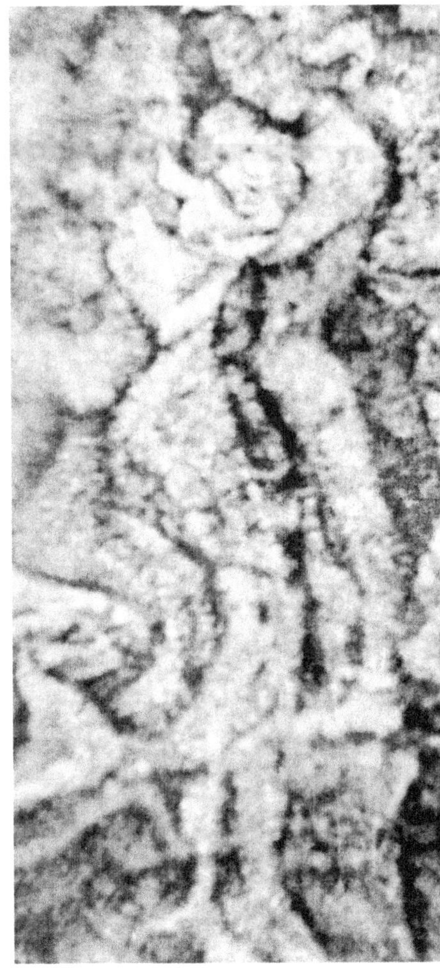

Above: One of Shaver's paintings of Merpeople, based on Rogfogo/Rokfoto imagery, from the book he created with Ray Palmer, *The Secret World* (1975).

WOODS

Green and strange are far vistas in the woods, the many layered beauty of the leaf-split light does lead the eye toward odd imaginings; sensualities allure in the distance, the far white trunks become the strangely turned bodies of desired women, forever fleeing, their forms dappled with the warm lights changing play.

Just beyond, always just beyond, one senses some great beauty waits to reveal the profound secret of life, to lay bare before your thirsty soul the very womb of mystery, the birth place of the seed of life.

THE ANGEL TREE-- PSALM TO A MAIDEN

Thy limbs are out-thrust lances of delight,
Thy fruit the breasts of daughters of divinity,
Thy buds a myriad gems of melody.
The white and waving hands of maidens are thy leaves.
The ripe red lips of life are berries on thy branches.
Breezes laugh and caress joyously all thy boing,
as though thy scent wore a delirious drug
That duped awareness into dreams of love's surprises.
Thy curving forms are the entangled, twining bodies of ecstatic lovers.
Thy blossoms are fecundity.

THE HOLLOW HILLS

The woman's neck has seven rings
And so has Venus, 'round her hill --
Her hollow hill, shaped like a breast;
The ringed hill of Venus
Where I lay and watched the blood
Beat through the rings 'round Venus' neck;
The Venus rings of soft-flowed flesh
That I caressed, when I was he
Who watched the bruise that he had made in love--
And now she slept.
Golden bangles hang and glitter dully
Upon the tapered base of this columnar throat;
Seven golden bangles--
And seven rings of flesh.
Flow love around and through flow love --
Seven times seven.
Burning is my body, and my eyes are fire.
Sleep lies upon her -- but for me
Is only waiting flame -- a desire
That is a death flames in me and with my fiery eyes
I caress that beauty -- for beauty burns me!
I cannot enwrap it, cannot make beauty into me,
Cannot own it;
Only see and burn.
Flaming are my veins like trees in wind,
Flaming trees of grouting blood that races in and out
Of a heart that cannot hold the beauty
But does let go!
I grasp the woman's neck--
The bangles jangle dully,
The seven rings of beauty empurple in my grasp.
I would seize beauty in my hands,
But only do I
Throttle Venus
Who was sleeping
Now is dead.

THE MYSTERY OF SHAVER

by Richard S. Shaver

The real "Mystery" of Shaver is that anyone had sense enough to publish it. Actually, it is a five-foot shelf of books in its entirety, so for as little as one expects it to be, it's amazing to most.

It is all about pre-first fall cultures. It is the true ancient history of our race before it was destroyed, and it is about WHAT HAPPENED TO THE SCIENCE AND TECHNOLOGY AFTER THE DESTRUCTION.

The Shaver Mystery began in the mid-1940s when I mailed Ray Palmer, then editor of Amazing Stories and Fantastic Adventures, an ancient Alphabet I had been working on for years. A is for animal, B is for baby, etc. In using it, one is really using the original ancient space-pidgin from which all language springs. It was brought to Earth in the first spaceships in the very beginning of things when the world was just starting to burgeon with a vast flora and fauna like nothing seen before of since. (In my record study, this was presaged by the first pass-over when spores and seeds were sprinkled over a totally sterile planet Just thawing from a long freeze, as though Earth had been a voyager Of deep space that had been captured by the Sun.).

You can figure out for yourself how this alphabet works with a few leads which I accidentally ran into long ago. You can trace words changed through the Age Of Ignorance after the Moon struck Earth, destroyed the ancient longterm culture and brought on the series of interim "cultures" we know as the Dark Ages. The latter were actually interim periods between moon-falls, none of which are as recognized or understood by so-called "science." Earth's history, back to the first moon-fall when our planet collided with the Moon when both orbiting the Sun, has been only dark and weary ages of little but war and ignorance and universal death every few thousand years as the Moon bounced off of our world again and again to take up a new orbit with the velocity acquired from Earth's spin.

At any rate, it was the alphabet that caught Palmer's eye and made him ask for a story based on its origin. I gave it to him and wrote more as long as they sold. It was not until later that I realized that Palmer's old writers had all been drafted, leaving him hard-up to get good stories. The man I succeeded was shot down over Germany.

No one, save for myself and a few in the underworld, had ever really understood the alphabet, though it is the actual bones of our own ancient tongue. Just' what it takes to grasp simplicity is simplicity itself, I guess. It's nothing complex — sound meanings persist intact while words change. One can recreate the ancient tongue just from studying the simpler sounds and their attached meanings. You can, it you can understand that it existed and that it came from space. We still speak the ancient tongue but have perverted and destroyed the real meanings built in. What we have done is what the politicians and militarists have done with their own jargon of un-meanings, made complex from the simple into non-meaning. We have made obscure that which was never meant to be obscure to anyone.

I cannot say that out of the millions who have read Shaver there were a dozen who truly grasped what I was trying to say. Ray Palmer least of all. I am always aghast at people asking Palmer for details about me, as he never got anything quite straight in this regard since I knew him. I have, for instance, no time for the occult viewpoint.

Spiritualism and so forth — and yet "Warning to Future Man," the very first story he bought from me, was changed to "I Remember Lemuria," which appeared in the March, 1945 issue of Amazing Stories and was later published between hard covers by Venture Books. The whole slant of everything I had to say was switched from the factual to the misty umbrella of spiritualism and reincarnation — utter hokum to me.

Deros and Teros and Shaver 's alphabet are real, actual physical blood and stink and awful flesh and nightmare in fact, but when Palmer got through with it,, it was all turned around into the dream world of mystical and the real/unreal religious fol-de-rol which never sees a fact as relative to anything like another fact. Nothing I ever wrote suggested any such idea; Palmer was just that sort of editor and I have struggled with it from the first.

I never felt as if what I really wanted to do was ever done. It's like digging in ashes, which is what I mean by mental tamper and telaug rule making our history and our literature by blocking off one's mind as one works. But, as you may have noted in Ted White's answer to my letter in the November, 1971 issue Amazing Stories, people either lie about it out of fear or else actually don't know that it exists at all.

I think they lie, just as Palmer would lie if the publisher asked him if he really believed in all of this stuff. He would say what seemed expected. I think a lot of these people KNOW something about the telaugmentive interference set-up whether they call it "marvs" or some other word, these days one can hear it whispered about quite frequently. But nobody comes right out in the open with it out of fear — a universal fear of it.

You could poll a whole countryside and every single person would lie that he didn't know what you were talking about. Over a campfire in the evening on a hunting trip of wherever else they feel really isolated and therefore safe from criticism, the same people will tell tales of phenomena that raise your hair. And every single tale includes mind reading, apparitions, voices and sounds of music in the wilderness when there was no living source in sight.

Earth is in truth ruled by the same ancient telaug system that ruled it in pre-Deluge times. Most people know it some of the time when it affects them; they hear it, frequently and tearfully. That is what Shaver writings are about. The cavern of the underworld exist. Buried cities exist. In them, hermetically sealed by the mud flows of upheaved ocean bottoms when the Moon struck us over and over again, is the vast treasure of a vast multitude of vanished populations, the treasures of a planet with a thriving space commerce. This is where the saucers come from and where they go; this is where they were found and re-operated recently.

All this is what Shaver tried to say as "fiction" even as H. G. Wells tried to say it in The Time Machine to wake modern Eloi to their peril.

THE CLOUD PAINTER

by Richard S. Shaver

Once there was a man called the Dawn Master. It was his job to supervise the painting with clouds at dawn as the whole world watched the sun come up. That long ago, the world turned much faster on its axis than it does today. They had three dawns to our one, and you didn't have to get up early to see the sunrise.

Cloud-painting was done with ionized beams of energy that caused the clouds to become denser or less dense according to the charge placed on the water droplets. Thus one could manipulate the colors of reflected sun- light and cause them to coalesce or to disperse, according to how the ionizing beam was moved about.

In those days the Dawn Master was chosen for the job of making the dawns more beautiful and soul-satisfying, and of all the artists in the world, the Dawn Master had the most critics and the most loyal devotees. For everyone had their own ideas about how the dawn painting should be handled.

Now, you may not think cloud-painting was a very important governmental task. In our world, so devoted to bustling and "industry," the dreamer who spends his time gazing at clouds is considered a wasteful and idle fellow.

But in that time, gazing at clouds was considered a necessary food for the soul. They were a people very devoted to things like art and poetry, and the colored shapes of changing clouds were considered the highest form of poetry combined with art, for to them each shape was a symbol of great inherent meaning.

In that time, bustling and doing things for the sake of doing, without proper thought as to the ultimate beneficence to the race and to the Mother Earth, was very much frowned upon. You see, they had had their fill of mass production and organized industry and had passed laws against all industry devoted to the benefit of a single man or group of men at the expense of other people's welfare and livelihood.

So being busy was no virtue unless one were busy with the general welfare. Cloud painting was considered a very necessary office of government, because so very many people all over the world benefited from the ritual of beautiful forms and shapes that had to be always new and different and very symbolically informative.

For in those days they had one fundamental law rigidly enforced. That law was thus: "Nothing Twice Alike!"

They enforced that law rigidly because it provided work for everyone. It ruled out the auto- mated factory, repetitively putting every artisan out of work, and allowed artistic individuality to flourish.

In those days they didn't allow artists to starve. They needed them desperately, for the law "Nothing Twice Alike" made it imperative that each article manufactured be separately designed. And only a real artist can design every single thing new and different and never twice alike. Artists were sought out and paid more by far than other workers.

So you can be sure that the Dawn Master did a lot of homework making sure that he never produced the same dawn twice, for he would have been reduced to workman status immediately.

To preserve his office for all the days of his 1,000-year-long life term, the Dawn Master had invented the computerized art form of design that could NOT produce the same design twice over, just to be on the safe side. Secretly at night he ran his computer overtime, devising and checking and figuring that the basic themes he put into the computer always contained a new element, so that the resulting design would be different from any other dawn in history.

Actually, after a long time at his job, the Dawn Master had grown aware that Mother Nature did a pretty good job of painting herself, so all he really did was to introduce into the computerized beam-mech a new element that would cause the result to be different than ever before. This was not so difficult as trying to oversee, all of the round the clock painting as the Earth rotated. Nobody could keep up with it otherwise.

There is no element of accidentalism in computer art, but then too there was no way a Dawn Master could control all the six points of the world compass all at once. He had to turn some of it over to the computer-art-board-beamdirector- complex.

But the general public thought the Dawn Master devised all those spectacular rosy formations of wonder all by himself. If they had known the truth, they would have thought much less of his art, and this was a worry to the Dawn Master, who had devised the art computer out of sheer necessity.

But his daughter knew. Aurora (named after the dawn goddess) was very worried about her dadda ...er...father, because in recent years he had become quite sloppy and went about in an old black tunic and skull cap. He wasn't the only artist that was ever careless about his personal appearance, of course, but he was the only one that had a curvaceous daughter only 200 years old to worry about him.

In that time, clothes were a fetish and ritual in themselves, and the most glorious artists were those who designed the most fantastic clothing. You see, there was a kind of creeping sybaritism in the social fabric that was mainly disguised as "Care and Cleanliness and Fantasy in Clothing."

But I can hardly explain that a foot-tall turban was not unusual, or that it might be arranged to represent other than totally mundane utility. Not anymore than I can explain that women wore tinkling bells on their ankles and were often tattooed totally to represent snake-skin, or insect beauty, or most anything an artist could represent...and those artists were people who spent centuries learning their art.

Tattooing was an ancient art that had once been very utilitarian, in that it was used mainly for camouflage. For Earth was very warm of climate, the weather machines holding the temperature stable with only slight variations. So a tattooed warrior, naked, was so designed skinwise as to be able to step into a bush and become indistinguishable from the leaves.

Then, as times grew equable, such things as war vanished from the world scene. All government functions were accomplished by wide-field mental-impulse augmentation, which ruled out the unruly passions of war so that no one could even think about making war, let alone actually do it.

With police work thus reduced to a minimum, the world became a place where camouflage was no longer needed, and tattooing evolved into an art of embellishment of the human form like nothing you can imagine from today's vulgarities.

I can't really tell you how the tattooed lady looked, for we have nothing of equal beauty to compare her with. But the Dawn Master, privately, would have confessed that he had taken more than one motif for a dawn theme from the backside of a woman he saw in the street!

The Dawn Master's real name was Peri-ton. There was a lot more of it because in those days families liked to know who they were related to and tacked them all on...but I can't pronounce the rest. Peri-ton meant a "Weighty Fairy" if translated, but they didn't think about fairies like we do. A "Peri" was a master of the art of magnification and optics, and ton meant something like "top-flight" in our modern words.

In those days fairies weren't thought of as unreal or mythical. They all knew the fairies were an extraterrestrial race who had spent a lot of time and work educating Earth races. So the Dawn Master's name really meant he had some extra blood in his family lines. But mostly his friends called him Perry, and his daughter, even though she was 200 years old and still growing, called him Dad.

Peri-ton was nearly 900 years old, but he was not very big for his age. Many people of his age ran 15 feet tall. Peri-ton was only around 9 feet tall, and Aurora was less than six feet tall, but she would be growing for a long time yet.

Anyway, some poking busy-body had learned about his computer and was gossiping about it. So Perry was worried more than usual about losing his job. In those days a job was a lifetime affair unless somebody was able to prove in court that ethics had been violated.

It wasn't any big thing, except that in the case of top-flight political figures like Peri-ton, exile was usually included in the court judgment. This was to avoid friction and punitive eventualities. And Peri-ton liked his life and his job and his place in the scheme of things.

Computerized art was not unknown, but like automated production of things for the people, it was frowned on as putting artists out of work. It was very like a union musician taking a non- union job; it could have wide repercussions.

And his use of the computer was out of sheer necessity. Nobody human could come up with a new dawn design for every 8- hour day, 728 days every year. But could he prove it? Would they listen?...or would they give him a summary trial that depended on the rules alone—rules never intended to be applied to a job like his? Rules and laws were all very well, but they didn't always precisely fit every circumstance. And in those days there was a very strong overlay of lawfulness and rule-keeping impulsion being broadcast from every ro-mech round the world. It was this overlay conscience that was causing Peri-ton's nervousness, and this in turn was causing a lack of attention to his appearance.

He was really a very good-looking man, with a strong aquiline face and a pointed black beard with really awe-inspiring mustaches. But when he didn't shave for a week he was a pretty hairy Peri.

This is how things were when Aurora really put it to him: "Dada," she said, "why do you use a computer to design your pattern layouts for the cloud painting? You do such lovely work of your own inspiration!"

Dada . . . er . . . I mean Peri-ton paused at his key-punching and grinned at Aurora a little sheepishly. "You see, daughter, I can't be sure I won't duplicate some pattern I used as a basic theme a century or two ago. Only by using this art-computer with its banks containing all previous pattern layouts can I be sure I haven't duplicated. You know the law. 'Nothing Twice Alike ' is particularly applicable to dawn painting. The only way I can keep the law is by breaking the unwritten law against machine art. It is an insoluble enigma for me...and I have kept it under wraps so long it smells a little. It will be a relief when it comes out in the open.

"Night- soil!" said Aurora. "That's a pretty kettle of fish! It hadn't occurred to me you were on the hob either way you jumped."

(You have to understand that in that time, they composted every bit of manure, and "night- soil" referred to the soil they used to soak up the refuse in the night...about on a par with "kitty litter" to us. It really wasn't much of an oath. But then the people of that day hadn't much to swear about, as they had conquered most of the problems that are beginning to look insoluble to us today.)

So the time came when a large scroll was presented to poor Peri-ton, calling him before the weekly tribunal (which was very like what we call a grand jury of citizens). All his suspected duplicities in art matters were listed in order of importance, even down to his composing of each and every date for the past year.

Anyway, poor Peri-ton had to explain at great length that although he did in fact use the computer, he had to break one law to keep another.

Now, it so happened that the Tribunal, purposely chosen from among the artists of the land, almost immediately broke into open discussion of the merits of this method, and this argument was in direct contradiction to every law of the land, for they were supposed to discuss, but not to argue heatedly. So what happened to Peri-ton became subordinated by what happened to the Tribunal, who had come together to crucify computer art and Peri-ton together, but found themselves locked up for the grievous crime of punching one another.

That was very understandable, for their feeling against machine art was very old and very important to them. No machine could ever compare with the virtuosity of the "real" artist — their living and their employment depended on that fact. Yet, even they could not bring Peri-ton's dilemma into any agreement with sense as they saw it. The conflict was just as insoluble to them as it was to him.

This was a famous story in that time of poets and artists and quiet everyday living in which dawn-watching was a ritual with all people who valued their beings and their minds and their talents. The dawn was sacrosanct. Yet. they could not see how Peri-ton could be condemned for keeping the law of "Nothing Twice Alike" by breaking the unwritten law against all machine repetition.

So, like all contradictions, the whole thing was quietly brushed under the rug or dumped into the nightsoil container and left to compost itself into less of a problem. It was all very distressing, particularly when the Tribunal found it had to pay the fine of 80 drachmas for riotous behavior. And 20 times 80 drachmas was no small sum.It was a quiet time, that age of the Dawn Master who used a computer against all the consciences of all the artists and won his case.

It was a quiet story about a quiet time when people were masters of their environment and had time to argue about how the dawn should be painted.

Richard Shaver. Photo by Richard Toronto

THE PEOPLE OF YESTERDAY: THE GIANT RACES OF THE PAST

by Richard S. Shaver

There are three main races now vanished forever from earth. There were the giant races, who left some enormous artifacts and ruins. There were the Mers, or ocean going, waterdwelling races of man. And there were the Amazons, who were not really "women" as we know them today, but were a Spartan race, very handsome but strong as men and as hard to understand socially as any artifacts on earth.

The giant races were NOT main-stream racial strains of earth men. Their teeth were very different, they lacked canines...although some of them look a lot like men of today, there were some very important differences.

The Mer races seem to have been our immediate forebears and look like us except for the fact they didn't emerge from the oceans and take up land life. They stayed in the oceans.

The Amazons had their own social structure, very close-knit and military, like the Spartan...but males of the sort we call male today only entered the Amazon strongholds on certain seasonal occasions. So that Amazons of the latter time were really two sorts...the male groups lived apart (just as some Polynesian and Malaysian tribes have their long houses for men and keep apart from the women and kids.)

These three main races , separate and distinct from the main stream of bi-sexual humanity, had their areas and their tribes and their cities. Whole continents acknowledged the rule of the Amazon armies. And great areas were inhabited by the giant races.... and the smaller races were kept out. And the oceans were the domain of the Mer people, even in myth and legend it is acknowledged that the oceans were the realm of Poseidon or Neptune or whoever happened to the the Sea King.

Today we think of all that weird set of names and shapes and thoughts as "Myths" to be ignored. BUT once they were the true shape of reality itself.

The forest races are harder to trace, as they only show up in the rock books made by the other races.

They lived in tree houses in the endless forests, and there were several kinds, probably including the remnants we now think of as the Yeti. There were white apes and dog apes like the modern baboon. These seem to have had a much more organized and "civilized" way of life than they do today, but it's hard to pin down in the fragmentary pictures.

There were also the flying apes... who were really akin to bats and had a bat-like nose...and would glide down like flying squirrels to attack most anything that moved below the giant trees where they nested in large numbers.

There are a great many such things now extinct that show up in rock books, but to TELL anyone about it is like telling about the picture of Cyrano de Bergerac and the woman in the moon... rather difficult when they have been seeing it every month without anyone noticing it.

The whole subject is like that, obscured only by the average Joe's lack of observational talents.

The forest races included some very long-tailed people, with hair-lips and fluffy tails and other quite unhuman characteristics. But they also included some of our very best strains of humankind... and to sort them out at this late date is like trying to climb a giant tree...they didn't leave many around.

So I don't try, I nurse my rock images and worry about man's future on his present course of total extinction for all thins I love, including the beauty of mankind.

So I keep saying "There are rock books in quantities which can easily resolve all the "anthropological controversies" if anyone can be bothered dirtying their clerical pinkies with them. Otherwise don't bother me with your pantywaist wool.

Anybody at all can prove this for himself by actually using some genuine workaday effort on looking at rocks with lens and light and genuine observation. But you cant do it with wordy wool, and you can do it by assuming "accidentalism."

SEA PEOPLE

To me, the most attractive residents of that bright original Eden were not the giants, not the "littles", not the tailed people of the forests. Not even the gloriously lovely Amazons.

The most attractive and most active were the Mers, the water people. Their name has come down to us as a synonym for beauty... the Mermaid.

In their portraits they are always in motion, flashing, through the white water like human trout, curving their long limbs in impossible feats of flexible strength and speed... raw power an utter poetry in motion.

A white water human, except when they sprawl in their impossibly fantastic beauty of iridescent fins and mottled sculptural form on the beaches or on the rocks like some idealized group of impossible seals!

Eventually you will see colored photos of these long-limbed Mers from the rock books they made of themselves.

In my reproductions , my necessarily limited methods of enlargement do not carry over the iridescence and the vital movement.

Did you ever try to paint a moving trout?

Even with perfect photo enlargement on canvas, I simply cannot get the color and the movement right.

No living artist could, but some exist who could do it infinitely better than I, or at least I hope so. I like to think it was those lovely log-powered Mers who survived the first terrible moon arrival. In those terrible times of whole oceans pulled from their beds and whirled round the :world under the arriving moon...they swam on and on and on... and survived somehow the crushing weight of the falling oceans returning to their beds.

Survived and gloried in their strength as they swam out the terrible rush of the mile-high tides to survive some of them. Just to survive in spire of the rushing-~ vastness and crushing weight of miles of ;water falling ever falling on them.I like to think it was the Mers who survived to once again eMerge on land to father a new race of landdwellers. I like to think it was the Mers who were our true earth born ancestors. To me the legendary Mermaid was the REAL EVE.

So I like to think, and so it can seem from some rock pictures.

Since this view does not jibe with Velikovsky's 5,000 year last flood... we have to place the second eMergence of the Mers on to land away back. after the FIRST fall, or after the most disastrous of the several moon collisions that so obviously, took place.

This survival of the Mers in their natural element, as the only members of man's nuMerous races of the past to survive and finally to sire the ancestors of our own land race... I base mainly on their appearance.

THEY LOOK LIKE US!

There are even Black Mers who look like us, like modern Negroes, and they are black and beautiful if you think that way.

They are certainly a different strain of fish-man, as different as trout are different from catfish. Different habits and a different way of life...but let's not get into all that.

The field is big enough , what with tailed people, midget people, giants and Mer-men and queer long-necked big-eyed creatures... like us yet so unlike us they could not be direct ancestors. You can see what Mers looked like in the photo of the moon fall rock on page...

You really begin to learn about rock books when you begin to look at your own photographs of them. This stage took me 10 long years to reach, before I finally acquired a good camera and some close-up equipment.

Up to this time I had not realized a set o bellows CAN be used in cropping. That's when you have a print made of a photo of a square inch of rock and then put that print in front of your bellows and make an equally enlarged photo of a square inch of print... you are really only then beginning to reach the kind of magnification needed to SEE what is there in the small text of the book.

These photos of photos turned out to be the best photos I had, and I began to realize that a camera can be a big aid to the eye in framing as well as enlarging certain areas of significance. There is one thing about a photo or a rock they hold still. I hadn't realized I could take a photo of such great magnification with only a few hundred dollars worth of equipment.

Now I knew, and this possibility of getting photos of the things I was able to see in my rocks opened the door for me to really rescue the vast library of the ancient world...without relying on help from the reluctant cult of "Scientists" I had so far been unable to contact. I had come to believe there was in fact no such genuinely sensible men of science able to discuss the optical problems or anything else about a "Mere" rock.

I sincerely hope such men exist, but I sincerely doubt it.

AMAZONS

(Every "great" scientist , particularly in this field of prehistory, has his special theory to espouse.)

Let me tell you what I think about the Amazons, whose beauty and martial renown come ringing down the empty halls of pre-history in spite of all the destruction and in spite of the theoreticians and misinterpreters of data.

THE AMAZON in the pictures in the rocks, went about with one large and lovely breast protruding and ,with the other one ... a veiled scar. Or at least historians think there was a scar there the nipple had been burned .when she was a child. BUT I suspect they were wrong on their theory and assumptions on that one too. I think the Amazon was true half-man half-woman and never had more than one breast in the early time.

The Amazon, in the pictures in the rocks, rent about in a scanty war-harness with one large and lovely breast out in the open. Where the other one should have be, there is in the pictures a sort of veil or apron depending- from the crossed strap of her harness. It was a small veil and about the only part of her body that was covered apart from the kilt ... which was shorter than the Scotch kilt. But had one thing in common with the Scotch .kilt. There was a Sporran hanging- from the waist belt. But it was NOT a pock t book. It was a lingam, a male organ in carved ivory.

Other Amazon outfits wore other totem signs than the carved male organ. But most of them contained some male connotation, some symbolism meaning ..."I am male, or better than male.. I am Amazon!"

Their harness was of black leather; and at the rump were ostrich feathers...at least they looked like Ostrich plumes... and a few plumes on the Grecian-looking helmet was the whole of her garb.

Helmets were fairly ornate metal shells... with eye-holes for pulling down over the face in battle, and they were worn upthrust on top of the head except in battle. They looked like fierce fighting faces of metal, highly engraved with curlicues and some inset gems.

The Amazon carried a very long, spear. .She had a need for it, for in Amazon tactics the phalanx. which we think of as Greek was a paramount tactic. Spears were grasped by several hands in the rear ranks and would stop a horse when so held.

Amazon war parties carried many wagon loads of other gear into battle. Studying such pictures one can't help but think; the Amazons were a product of an interim age, and not the original peaceful age of the first pre-moon time.

One piece of this war gear that interested me was the huge bow mounted on wheels. A cross-bow of mammoth proportions, it had very intricate sighting, equipment, a plumb bob with the cord crossing a set of numbers that gave them elevation and level horizon ..and a spring attachment the bow-string, passed over gave them calibrated TENSION... translated into yardage.

It looked wry much as if a warrior familiar with the gear could put that 10 foot long arrow into a fly's eye 200 yards or so. Was that huge wheeled -cross-bow destined to bring`: down mammoths used as war-animals It could have done the job.

Amazons were NOT pussy-cats. They were a warrior people, operating on Spartan upbringing. In war as in peace, the Amazons were called "Fear-Ladies" in the few writings about them I have worked on.

The phrase gives one the feeling they inspired in the helpless or luckless peoples who opposed them.

The Amazons ruler, or war chief is often down on many rocks, a kind of universal symbol. She as a powerful and very large matriarch with a scar down one cheek very like a Heidelberg saber scar. In many pictures this cheek is also covered with a little veil as is the missing breast.

She sat on a throne covered with furs, and flanked by a huge bird that looks very much like a condor. The Condor or gigantic eagle was one of their main symbols, and one runs into it often.

Their schools were symbolized by a gigantic EGG of stone, which was topped by this huge bird's head carved in stone.

One can imagine the school for young Amazons as most anything but what it was... a fine military academy which raised the kids from a very young age to adulthood.

Amazons were very good looking people, but they were not in later years what they were in the beginning... a one-sexed creature that could reproduce itself...that is, a self-fertilizing creature able to reproduce all by its lonesome.

Somewhere along the line, sex reared its head... and I suspect it came about because of their habit of taking captives and impressing people into their service. But let's leave the speculation on sex and its consequences and mental quirks to the "scientists" We are only intent upon what can be learned from the rocks they left behind.

They are lovely female creatures in their pictures, and their art surpasses most other rock books. So one can't say...they were some sort of freak of the far past who reproduced without copulation. One suspects they are the original sea-animal who fathered and mothered us all in the dim past...and the INTERIM race we now call Amazon .as a lacer survival of the original... model which died out a gain as the two sexed race became more nuMerous.

Anything one has to say about it is guess work. One can only voice one's deductions from the few intact and perfect pictures one can find showing, organs of both sexes in one body...and on, can't be one isn't handling some medical essay in stone rather than a universal model.

I suspect the: original Amazon was just such an able and -marvelous creature who mothered us all, once. But it is all a long time ago.

However, the fact that boys have nipples and girls have similar vestiges of male organs should give one the perspective...once upon a time men and women were one and the same thing in one body.

I am not alone in this suspicion mankind's beginnings.

They were lovely and strong and capable and one finds their stories in many places. "Amazon stone" among rock hounds is a green stone of good quality...but Amazons stone to ME is a rock of spectacularly high quality of art content.

That I think the Amazon had one breast by natural causes and were dual sexed...like Christine Jorgensen and similar cases the doctors fuss over. I suspect such people are NOT freaks at all, but Merely throw-backs to the original pattern of this human race.

Which should make them all feel somewhat better about being in this modern world of intolerance and other foolishness.

They did NOT remove one breast by surgery as our so-correct history texts sometimes tell you.

They never had one!

However, some pictures show them recruiting army trainees from among young people in the villages. How, it seemed to me that in these recruits to their armies the breast of the YOUNG was seared in youth and never grew because of this treatment!

It was their sign and symbol...the one-breasted armies of the Amazons are a part of our legends . And our legends are the ONLY historical remnants we have that contain ANY truth about the early time.

It has been fairly well established that the Froesian empire which preceded the Germanic empire :as an .Amazon outgrowth... or- successor to the original Amazon. From all I could gather, the Amazons ruled both coasts of the Atlantic at one time... previous to the last catastrophe. They were not a small group of ladies inhabiting the back: woods. They were IT, the best-looking, the best organized, the best-dressed and most literate of all the post-deluge racial groups.

It is quite probable, too, that when Hercules actually wrestled with the living, genuine Hippolyta, he lost the match.

So don't sneer at the Christine Jorgensens. They are as natural, or more so, than ourselves.

One scene I painted of Amazon war, showed the fear-ladies with stem powered swamp buggies equipped with both stern wheels and caterpillar treads, amphibious steam powered vehicles.

With that sort of technology, building amphibious swamp crawlers with seats for 30 or 40 warriors, they were NOT a backwoods outfit. You see them charging uphill against a rain of spears with a string of war elephants awaiting them at the top of the hill.

Apparently fear ladies didn't have any, they just handed it out. On each thigh was a short sword strapped to the front of the thigh, like no other way of wearing a sword I ever saw. And on the middle of their back was the long sword with the hilt projecting above the shoulder. They also had a holstered weapon of quite peculiar look like a big candle stick...whether it was the legendary flame-sword or a percussion type I could not decide.

They carried the legendary crescent shield, all right, but otherwise, you can't recognize the Amazon of legend in the actual pictures of them. They looked more like black paint Greek figures on vases then anything else I can compare them to, yet with so many variants it's hard to describe them. Their crest was plumed but pointed, not curved like the Greek.

In one picture of the Amazons on the march, the leader of the march was a good head taller than the others...and preceded by a tracker who had on leash two dog apes. Neither dog nor ape, they looked like baboons... yet with a definite air of greater intelligence than the baboon of today. But then, so many of these pictures give one the impression of more favorable mental al climate then today.

I believe the Amazon dominated the central sea of North America... as well as the Atlantic coast. .And that in relatively recent times... just previous to the last world deluge. But it's only an impression.

The Amazon culture rose upon the ruins of an earlier world. One can find Amazon pink stucco on top of older carved door lintels giving rise to the speculation...did the Amazons redecorate the old structures with the same passion as our modern interior decorators?

So don't go despising interior decorators for being a bit feminine. Under that trim exterior there probably beats a warrior's Spartan heart superior to the wholly masculine ideal.

He-she was ONCE a dominant form of life on this planet, and they ruled half the world with an iron hand in a velvet glove is hardly disputable, if you check the record.

But what is more to the point is the discovery that he-she is a "natural" type and not a freak of' nature. The very earliest stones ~ could find showed this bi-sexual he-she running things s with a high hand, a r c of people quite distinct fro ~ our modern two-sexed society.

It ray very well be that races with two sexes as things are organized today is strictly a "modern" development, and things weren't all that way in the ancient first time of life on the planet.

It could well be that the Amazon is the "natural" original life form of human who both fathered and mothered her own children.

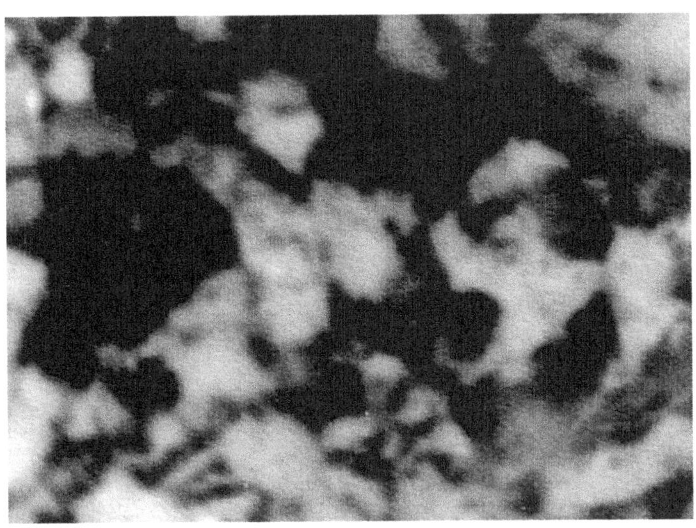

ARTICLE BY RICHARD SHAVER FOR THE FANZINE *VAMPIRE #6*, JUNE 1946, EDITED BY JOE KENNEDY.

EDITOR'S NOTE: Since much has been written in the fan press against the Lemurian series in Amazing Stories, we believe it is no more than fair that Dick Shaver be given the opportunity to tell his side of the story. We are completely convinced of the author's sincerity , although the following article does not necessarily reflect the views of Vampire's staff.)

Up to twelve years ago I was a stf fan, much like yourself, I suppose. I thought I knew exactly what was true in science and what could happen and that I could draw a precise line in my reading between fact and fantasy.

Then it happened, almost exactly as I tell it in the stories I write. Things that couldn't happen except through a wonder-science never produced by modern men of science at all.

There were three conclusions. The first that these machines and rays came from space (visitors). the second was that they were modern secret science -- things that science had developed and leapt to itself as a monopoly, for the power and wealth the advantages of using these apparatuses would give them. This second conclusion was my conclusion until I knew more about it, which took many years. It is the usual deduction of the person first contacting secret ray.

The third deduction came after long experimentation with the phenomena I talk about in my stories. That this thing was a persistence of the same thing the medievals were talking about when they raised such a hullabaloo about witchcraft. The same thing Homer was talking about when he mentioned the immortal gods. I did a lot of research, believe it or not. And this last deduction is the correct one. The caverns I saw were not modern -- they were not even built fairly recently by space travelers who stopped here long enough to leave such a gigantic traces-- were built before man had a history. they are the big missing portion of history, and they have a history all their own far more important in many ways than our own surface history.

Witchcraft, fairy tales, legends of the underworld --are not all antique fiction. It is surprising how well they describe some things that are done with machines. Merlin, in King Arthur, had a cave full of machines; and he died in it. In Deirdre--a ray from nowhere cuts down the heroes at the climax. the list of references is endless -- I know -- I looked them up. Take "The Destruction of Da Derga's Hostel" -- a fifth century Irish mss. -- translated in the Five Foot Shelf -- The Men from Elfmounds are mentioned over and over. The underworld was well known in the past and it shall be in the future. It has been the monopoly of a little group of savagely monopolistic people for a few centuries.

Read Lovecraft's rewrite for a woman friend of his -- "The Mound" in *Beyond the Wall of Sleep*, quite a long story and as good a picture of the underworld as I ever read.

Take off about twenty percent of Lovecraft's weird ideation and ornamentation -- and you have an exact picture of the underworld -- except for the radioactive light.

As for *Maxin 96* (The Lemurianist fanzine -- ed.) I find it unfortunate that all the occultists have leaped to my banner -- for I never meant to infer that spirits had anything to do with what I am talking about. In fact the ray phenomena I mention explain away all spiritualist phenomena as ray work -- of my despised dero -- incidentally -- the real explanation of all evil is dero, detrimental energy robot. These mysterious ray phenomena do exist and occur regularly. I always thought it was wool and lies and fakers myself just as you probably do -- 'till they happened without benefit of a medium within miles. No, I didn't leap to the conclusion that they were spirits. I figured out the real reason-- and it is some answer. Naturally it is hard to swallow offhand, mainly because you don't get all the background. Read "Da Derga's Hostel" and Lovecraft's "The Mound".

I note in Vampire how the fans booded me at the convention in Newark. All this active fan opposition hurts like hell - hit the truth of it is -- <u>if</u> they UNDERSTOOD! But they are not my worst worry. My worry is the mad dero of the caverns -- and they do our country even more harm. Some of those fans who are most loud in denouncing my "LIES" are directly used by the dero ray for that purpose. <u>DON'T BE USED</u>! The very copulation by which those same fans were conceived was watched over a telaug by a dero or a tero -- humans who inherit a long line of conditional variational factors form a surrounding entirely different from our own -- was watched for the vicarious entertainment received from the augmented emotional and sensory impulses which is greater than ordinary human.

Under our feet is a world of scientific wonder beyond any writer's power of description, built there before earth had a sun. Those metals don't rust -- those caves are as dry and hot as a desert -- perfectly preserved, they wait for modern scientist will accept this "impossible" truth is the only stumbling block between men and a wonder world. Our race was not the only race on earth; there were greater races and greater times. We are in truth the degenerate descendants of a great race, and not the ape's mutant brother evolutionists would have us think. If you had been to Mars on an unannounced trip --how would you tell about it? Prove it, people would say. Well, it's a hard job, but we may get it done -- this proof you want is growing every day. Pluto did live, and strangely enough Dante's concept of the nether world and the city of DIS has its counterpart in actuality.

::Richard Shaver

Above: The envelope in which Shaver sent the rogfogo packet and *This Tragic Earth* to Ray Palmer.
Below: The envelope in which Shaver sent his account of *"Dr. Soffice"* to Palmer.

THE SECRET CAVES OF THE DERO
FROM *MYSTIC MAGAZINE* #15, 1956.
THE SHAVER MYSTERY NO. 4 THE SECRET CAVES OF THE DERO
BY RICHARD S. SHAVER AS TOLD TO RAY PALMER

What do the Dero do? What would YOU do? if you were incredibly stupid, with your mind deranged by powerful augmented radioactive rays constantly beamed upon you by ray projectors originally intended to beam beneficial rays, but now perverted in their activity by being sunpolared — the rays they manufacture are detrimentally radioactive infected, and the rays they conduct from the surface, are multiplied in their poisons by the machines so that they are far more damaging than they are to us surface people.

You would find yourself in possession of many marvelous machines left by the Elder races, and you would use them in idle, childish play. You would use the telaug and vision rays to spy upon surface people, and you would use the projection rays to fool them with fantastic images, you would use the tractor rays to open railroad switches before speeding trains, you would even be so childish to trip people going down stairs, open manhole covers before them, and so on. You would use the marvelous surgical rays for the diabolical slicing of delicate nerves in the brain, or other parts of the body, to create mental and physical cripples. You would burst their hearts so that a "heart attack" would eliminate some important person and cause chaos in surface governments. You would do an almost fantastic number of things that could add up to the veritable "works of the devil"!

Except for one thing: you would risk retaliation from tero at equally powerful ray mechanisms... But occasionally, as some guard suffers a momentary lapse of vigilance, or has his attention diverted, you will be able to get in some quick deviltry, and you will howl with sadistic mirth at the result.

For you are mad! Madness in the caves is an almost universal condition. It cannot be otherwise, for more than one reason. First is the reason that you are exposed to ray damage much more extensive than is caused normally by the sun (and the moon — you've herd of the madness caused by Luna's rays, not a myth, and a superstition, but based on fact, for Luna's rays are only sun rays, polarized by reflection, and thus dangerous to a small extent). Moonlight and sunlight, conducted upon the dero cavern dweller by his augmenting apparatus, subject him to much more detrimental effect than on the surface.

The second reason is that the human mind (and the dero are as human as you and I) cannot stand too much torture without cracking; and torture is a part of the daily life of a dero. Few indeed have not at one time or another fallen into the power of a mad local despot and been subjected to unimaginable tortures besides which the Inquisition's devices are child's play.

A third reason, perhaps more effective, though more insidious, is the extensive and perverted use of the machine called "stim." The ancient purpose of this machine was to accentuate the pleasure derived from sex, largely by beneficial rays which restored energy as fast as it was dispensed; and also was a health machine, dispensing various nutrients and vitamins and minerals directly through the skin and into the body. The dero spend days at a time in these machines, indulging in an orgy of sex that, rather than being stimulating, is exhausting and detrimental because the stim machines are contaminated by radioactives and their good effects nullified and turned instead to bad effects. Because of them, recessive elements of heredity are accentuated, and a continual downward genetic scale is the result.

Yet, in madness there is craft! Incredible craft, and it is coupled with great secrecy. These degenerates aren't going to risk the pleasures that are theirs, by letting any surface people take them from them by force. Interlopers are slain (after torture), and secrecy is maintained at all costs. Because of the aid their machines give their mental processes, this craftiness is vastly multiplied, and it would take a clever surface man indeed to out-think them in the direction of subterfuge, etc. A vast curtain of error is continually hung before the eyes of surface man to conceal the truth of their existence. And it is an incredibly effective curtain. It is the most insidious propaganda imaginable, and involves hypnotic effects hard to believe. WAS that thought you just thought, your own! You would be absolutely certain it was yours, if you were certain there was no way for anyone else to think it for you. And it takes a great deal of experience to be able to see a thought for an alien thought, when it occurs in your mind. But it can be done. Question your thoughts with reason sometime, and see if many of them are not thoughts that would not have occurred to you in the natural reasonable course of thinking. Question your dreams, sometime. The effects of haphazard stringing together by your subconscious of your own personal, and sometimes long-forgotten memories? Ever have an incident in a dream come from something beyond your memory — honestly? Something you KNOW isn't anything you remember, because it was never before experienced?

Subtlety is here. And if entirely unsuspected, totally effective.

But to admit such things to a psychiatrist is to admit to mental derangement. To admit them is to risk admission to an insane asylum. So, here on the surface, the secrecy pattern is maintained, even by surface people. You yourself, if you hear a voice, can be and usually are, your own worst enemy!

How did I learn about caves? I've said it before. At first by an inadvertent contact, because I seemed to be "in the know." Then by contact with friendly tero, who, because I had accidentally gotten in on the secret , and seemed friendly, and harmless, and did maintain the secrecy, was allowed snatches of information and contacts that led to more contacts. Then some real tero friends who began to pass on to me knowledge that might make man a better man, and happier, just as they have for countless ages, sneaking bits of knowledge to men whom we revere today as the "discoverers" of great scientific principles. Nikola Tesla was such a man. Edison was such a man. Investigate for yourself the "mystic" overtones of each man's life! Read Edison's diary, and see how close he was to the borderline of admitting he heard voices, and that there were strange "psychic" sources for much of his knowledge. Read how Tesla invented things by simply "copying them" from actual visible and functioning projections hanging in the air before him! So it was with me, and they showed me much.

But then I broke the secrecy rule, and thereafter fled across the world, pursued by vengeful dero, sometimes protected, and sometimes not — and the "sometimes nots" have mostly destroyed any chance I've had to accomplish what I intended. Even my story was perverted into fiction, until it was a subject to ridicule.

Proof? You want proof? Having read this far, is it reasonable for you to DEMAND proof? Not very. Yet, there is proof. Everywhere you look! And I'll try to point those proofs out to you. Let me just speak my mind, with no regard to coherence or continuity, so that somewhere in the hodgepodge, you may seize upon some ammunition for thought, so that you may start thinking for yourself — the proof will appear, as effective proof as is possible to give.

You will see that I CAN "hand you" a machine! Machines you use every day. But you will ask that I hand you a "new" machine. Perhaps I CAN. Perhaps I shall! It has been said: "ask and ye shall receive." Exactly that has been known to occur before! Remember you any of these incidents? RECOGNIZE you any! Or was it God who answered your prayer! Or somebody else's prayer? But you HAVE observed it! Do you REMEMBER it! Letters in large numbers have accused me of implying this and meaning that — which I didn't. The confusion arises of course from the fictional treatment my message has had to be given.

Some readers have drawn quite a variety of erroneous ideas. Some of them are right. The truth is wild enough to suit anybody. But I wish to get the picture clearer for them.

One of the commonest errors is in the use the word "dero" has been receiving. Readers infer in their letters that all cavern people are "deros," that "dero" and "cavern dwellers" are synonymous. That is wrong! We wouldn't be alive if a large part of the people down there weren't fighting like hell for us and for themselves against the true "dero."

A dero is a cavern wight whose ancestors had the habit of bringing in the sunlight over the penetrays. Their evil nature is due to a constant "hearing" (telepathic) of sun vibrants because those same penetrays they use to bring in the sunlight and warmth were designed to handle thought-waves, to detect and augment waves of those frequencies heard by the brain. Their brains got dis (infections) on the lipoid films of the brain cells, where thought is generated. This went on for centuries, for an age, and the hereditary result was a dero, the ancient "Devil" of mythology, and his people —

humans whose minds handle only disintegrant pattern thought. ALL CAVERN PEOPLE ARE NOT DEROS, thank God.

The good ones do a lot of work for use, in subtle unseen ways, avoid tamper accidents by helping out a driver, get some doctor info on how to stop a plague, and are the source of some of our modern inventions by handing over suggestions to an inventor, unbeknownst, because they saw a similar device in the wreckage of the caves.

Even all the bad ones are not deros. A dero is an automaton of evil, and not an ordinary crook. He isn't that smart.

I am trying to say that our civilization is a sham! That our education is a very shoddy substitute for what it could be if the truth of our past were known.

I am trying to say that if we knew who and what some of our present-day bosses really were, we would be vastly worried at their apparent careless and oppressive attitude toward ourselves, the people — which attitude is shown in their deliberate deprivation of all science of the advantages that would arise from a general knowledge of and study of the rays and mech with which their rule is enforced.

They hold that they won't turn over the info, that it is like an atom bomb in importance, and they are keeping it in their own hands.

I reply that I wish they would because so many deros use it, too — and that they don't need to keep the WHOLE of that science a secret. So much of it is purely benevolent and medicinal. Truth is they are not educated, do not realize what they are doing in keeping the whole a secret still today.

I am saying there are millions of people besides Shaver who know there are vast caverns under earth, full of strange, miraculously potent machinery — and that they do not speak because it is so obvious that they would be misunderstood to the point of persecution.

There are many things I have heard that I do not know are facts. To mention these along with the things I know ARE facts causes an almost unavoidable confusion.

I have heard that surface light and power and coal are possessions of the ray-people. I don't KNOW it, I HEARD it. I have HEARD that some of them have harems of thousands of young women. I don't KNOW it. I DO KNOW they have harems, and an oriental contempt for all western morality — but because of the nature of social life developed around the sue of stim-rays, I can understand this different morality.

I KNOW many terrible things that I cannot find a way to tell except as fiction. These are things so lurid and impossible they are hard to make credible even in a lurid stf.* tale. They could not be considered as facts by and ordinary man, because he has not seen and could not accept. These are looked for by those who know something of the great secret, and look for recognizable information in the "forbidden" field.

I KNOW they have weapon rays that kill at fifty miles and more. That they HIT what they shoot at with these. A man cannot even think of such weapons without fear; still we must — and THEY HAVE BEEN WITH US right along.

I KNOW they have telaug beams that hear thought from a man's mind up to fifty miles and more. That is an extremely sensitive receiver, for the sending of one brain is not exactly powerful in voltage.

I KNOW they visit space, and receive visiting ships from space, some of which do not get away again. I don't know WHY they return to earth, for NO ONE HERE is getting a square deal.! The ships that return must belong to those who THINK they benefit from the repressive, throttling monopoly of all the good things of earth.

I am saying that earth's peoples are supporting a destructive, extravagantly luxurious and decadent "secret class" who rob us of our birth right — the science that could be learned from the mechanisms of the Elder race; which same mechanisms are the instruments that have held this class in power for many, many centuries.

I am saying that, due to many conditions which we cannot understand over a long period of time, many of these people are idiotic, and unfit to be allowed to continue as our "secret" overlords.

I say that if people generally knew this condition, they would lose the awe and fear that keeps from the race of man many great secrets which would prove a new and greater path of life for all of us.

I am saying to these men who cry "we want an artifact, and inscription, an ancient manuscript, we want proof!" — you HAVE proof all about you! But your minds are so slanted by wrong teachings that you misinterpret these artifacts and remnants on the surface which tell the truth about the God cavern's existence.

One either "knows" of the underworld or one does not. It is vey much like a seeing race with eyes living beside and among a race without eyes who refuse their existence. BUT WE ARE PRESENT AND WE DO SEE! (WE meaning those on the surface "who know.")

**STF = Scientifiction (i.e., Science Fiction)*

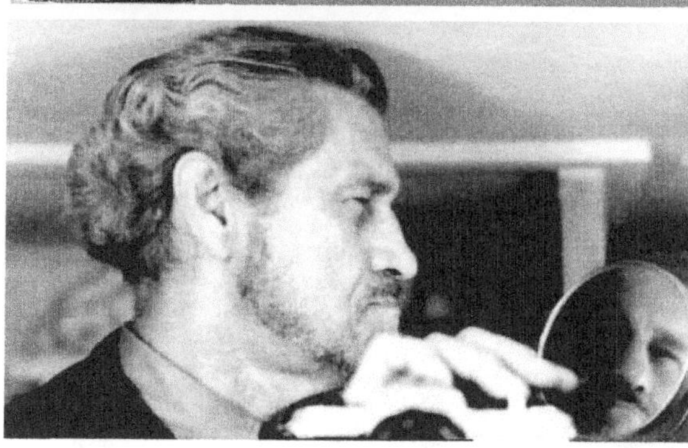

This book was compiled in memory of Richard S. Shaver, to the memory of his tumultuous, sometimes troubled life; his voluminous body of work; to the memory of his struggle for acceptance as an artist, writer, and philosopher, which never really came during his lifetime. Rest In Peace, R.S.S.

ABOUT THE EDITOR

Wm. Michael Mott (Mike to his friends) is a widely-published writer and artist who has five books and many magazine features in print. He's written about paranormal phenomena; comparative myth, religion and folklore; UFOs; cryptozoology; pulp, adventure, Sci-Fi and fantasy fiction; and art and education topics. He's been a featured guest on in excess of 30 national and internationally-syndicated radio programs, including Coast to Coast AM (3 times), and current he's one of the co-hosts at Unraveling the Secrets, a weekly program at Paranormal Soup Radio (www.unravelingthesecrets.com). His personal web site is http://www.mottimorphic.com and he also has a Facebook fan page out there somewhere (linked from the web site). He can be reached through the web site, or at wmmott@mottimorphic.com. He loves his kids and really, really likes books on myriad topics, dogs, and edged weapons. In addition to illustration work and writing, he crafts hand-made shillelaghs and walking-sticks upon occasion.

OTHER BOOKS BY WM. MICHAEL MOTT

For availability information on these titles, please visit:
www.gravedistractions.com/william-michael-mott.php

CPSIA information can be obtained at www.ICGtesting.com
Printed in the USA
LVOW03s2139100314

376788LV00020B/1504/P

9 780985 599157